CAVEMEN, MONKS, &SLOW FOOD

A HISTORY OF EATING WELL

DEVRA GARTENSTEIN

This book is dedicated to all
the creative, driven, quixotic
food producers in my life.

Contents

Introduction

ONCE HEARD AN interview with Jacques Pepin, the cookbook author who served as chef for three different French heads of state. He and the interviewer were discussing ways that one's tastes changed as one grew older, and the interviewer asked about his current favorite foods. Pepin answered, "Very good bread with very good butter."

It was such a simple answer, but on another level, it wasn't simple at all. Today we think of white bread as processed garbage, but refined flour was once an expensive status symbol. Once whole grain loaves were the main food source for struggling peasants; now we find them in natural foods stores and artisan bakeries. Bread riots precipitated the French Revolution. Other foods were available, but the people wanted bread. For them it was an inalienable right, their most basic food as well as an affordable luxury.

Everybody eats. We eat for survival, and we eat for pleasure. We choose foods for their taste; we also make eating decisions based on fads, taboos, and class conceits. Poor people have always wanted to eat the meals that rich people had on their tables. Aside from the allures of aroma and flavor, these delicacies also served as emblems of wealth and success. When sugar was a pricey luxury, rotten teeth were a status symbol.

The hunger for rare and expensive foods spurred a spice craze in medieval Europe as families spent fortunes for seasonings that grew halfway around the globe. Explorers lost their lives seeking direct routes to the Spice Islands, and countries fought wars to control strategic territories, monopolizing trade and reaping exorbitant profit margins. Their collective efforts destroyed many indigenous cultures and, for better or worse, birthed a new world unified by global trade and cultural exchange.

But the story of our connection with food is more nuanced than a simple tale of have-nots coveting rare and expensive treats. While chefs hired by kings and celebrities prepared sumptuous feasts, home cooks developed fine foods of their own. Farm wives, monks, and innkeepers coaxed optimum flavor and yield from whatever ingredients they could afford. In fact, home cooks have been so adept at preparing great food that the cultural elite have often ended up imitating *them*. According to the widely told tale, Brazil's national dish, *feijoada,* evolved from slave owners handing down pig parts they didn't want, like the ears and the feet. The slaves cooked these treasures with black beans, creating a dish that has become a national icon. Similarly, the French classic *pot au feu*, literally "pot on the fire," emerged from the peasant practice of keeping a pot simmering for days and throwing in whatever was available.

As a species we are predisposed to enjoy food. Our collective culinary canon, from the Amazon jungle to the halls of state leaders, represents a body of knowledge too vast to ever be catalogued and could very well be the most impressive thing we have ever accomplished. It includes the playful, sophisticated tinkering of molecular gastronomy and the oral catalogue of thousands of plant and animal species that keep hunter gatherers alive and happily fed.

Our diets have deteriorated dramatically during recent centuries, though there have always been cycles of abundance and need fueled by droughts and bad decisions. The current eating crisis features money hungry corporations owning the food system and aggressively marketing unhealthy products with high profit margins. The world's urban population has been steadily growing for centuries. Families who traditionally produced their own food using time-tested skills and community resources have had to find new ways of feeding themselves as their living environments and kitchen facilities have changed. Multinational food companies have eagerly stepped in to fill the void, designing and marketing an unending variety of highly processed convenience foods.

As a result of these changes, despite thousands of years of grassroots cooking traditions, we have largely forgotten what it means to eat well. We read books about nutrition but often make poor choices when we go to the grocery store. We are easily confused by seemingly contradictory information. The American media has made much of the so-called French Paradox, or the observation that French people have a lower incidence of heart disease than Americans even though the French eat heartily of foods linked to compromised cardiovascular health, such as meat, cheese, and butter. Perplexed nutritionists speculate as to how the French manage to stay reasonably healthy. Perhaps the tannins in their red wine fight cholesterol. Or maybe the French thrive because they take time to truly savor their food rather than wolfing it down while they're driving or between other tasks. Maybe they're healthier because they walk more or because the meat and dairy they eat come from healthier animals.

The American media sees the French diet as a paradox in part because we have grown accustomed to the idea that eating well involves a fundamental conflict between what we want and what we need. According to prevailing cultural assumptions, the food that tastes best is either unhealthy or expensive. But, as the French have shown, that is not necessarily the case. We do seem to be biologically predisposed to enjoy foods that are salty or sweet or high in fat, but our bodies are also capable of telling us how to eat well, once we learn to listen. When we eat too many of the wrong foods, we feel bloated. Over time many of us develop genuine aversions to foods that taste good but, in the end, bring more discomfort than pleasure.

Our confusion about what it means to eat well is further complicated by the fact that food scientists have grown adept at cheaply replicating many of the flavors which our bodies have evolved to crave. Foods that were once difficult to find are now available almost everywhere, and we are naturally disposed to reach out for them. As a species, we have spent dramatically more time foraging for edible plants than living in cities and shopping at convenience stores. For our ancestors, salt, fat, and carbohydrates were relatively hard to come by and necessary for their very survival. Manufacturers of processed foods have learned how to push these nutritional buttons without offering any real food value.

At the same time, their advertisers skillfully push our psychic buttons. By emphasizing the tension between enjoyable and healthy food rather than the qualities that they share, ads for convenience foods tickle our personal versions of a broader tension deeply embedded in our popular and intellectual culture. Much of traditional Western thought is based on the idea that there is a fundamental split between the mind, or the soul, and the body.

We see this divide in the idea of sexual pleasure as an animal impulse to be controlled by a rational psyche. The idea of unhealthy food as a sinful pleasure has similar roots and is just as useful to an advertising industry aimed at selling guilty indulgences.

Rich and decadent foods provide a sense of luxury, a reward for a hard day's work. This is true even when the products in question are mass-produced and not particularly luxurious. The convenience of fast food and the sweetness of candy offer easy, affordable pleasures. Their popularity is, in part, a consequence of a system where daily wage labor is rarely satisfying or rewarding. In this environment, it is profitable for advertisers to stress the pleasure of consuming unhealthy foods, contrasting it with the so called sacrifice of steering towards healthier options.

Consumer culture leads us to believe that we share an emptiness that can only be filled with purchased products. Great food that is also healthy challenges this idea. Corn on the cob is sweetest moments after you pick it, but unless you grow your own or know someone who does, you're unlikely to enjoy this experience. The same is true of most truly fresh foods: you can't eat bread straight from the oven or fish right out of a river unless you take the time to knead dough or sit with a fishing pole. Some restaurants and bakeries recreate these sensations and sell them as consumer products, but they cannot be mass-produced.

Perhaps the recent enthusiasm for good food is a stumbling step towards a deeper transformation, one that challenges prevailing consumer ideals and replaces them with more sustainable values. To be sure, this movement has been shamelessly commercialized, from designer gadgets and frozen entrees from distant cultures, to entire television networks devoted exclusively to culinary programming. But a genuine, widespread interest in good food could start to change the larger context in which our eating occurs.

A strong collective movement towards eating well rewards small and conscientious producers, who offer quality that their larger competitors cannot imitate. The acts of cooking or growing your own food use hours that are not spent working, or shopping, or watching television. The thriving market for well-crafted foods lets independent producers generate their own livelihoods, maintaining some degree of personal autonomy. Organic farmers save and rejuvenate land that would otherwise be depleted by factory farming.

It is exciting to see an emerging facet of contemporary culture that is good for us on many levels. It is especially encouraging to view it in a historical context, as a quiet revolution based on collective knowledge.

IN THIS BOOK, I will explore the ways that our eating habits and attitudes about food have changed through the ages, as well as common threads weaving our contemporary traditions into a very old fabric. This narrative tells the story of everyday foods as well as special meals. It describes our complicated feelings about the relationship between these very different styles of eating, from religious orders that shun meat to peasant cuisines that make so much out of so little.

I focus mainly on Western cuisines because they are the most familiar to me and because there is so much written material available about them. My own food experience emerged from the Jewish culinary tradition, which places family meals at the center of religious occasions. My parents fiercely disagreed about the place of religion in our home, but they shared a love for good food. During my adult life, I have owned a variety of food businesses, my favorite of which has been a farmers' market concession stand. I have been fortunate to be part of the local foods movement as it has grown and thrived. Working in this environment, I feel a connection to the countless people who have participated in market culture since the beginning of civilization, meeting in public places to exchange goods and stories. I start the book with an overview of what we know about how our earliest ancestors ate and what their food meant to them. This section spans a vast period of time, reaching back even before the emergence of our unique species, *Homo sapiens*. The next part describes the Neolithic revolution, when early cultures learned to farm. For them the question of what it meant to eat well must have been confusing, as they glimpsed the possibilities offered by their newfound capacity to change the landscape but found themselves enjoying a more limited selection of foods.

The following chapter explores the rise of early civilizations, which were made possible in large part by agricultural innovations which enabled communities to accumulate surpluses of grain. It took a certain degree of social organization to farm so efficiently, and in turn, the abundance they created benefitted some people more than others. We can trace the emergence of social stratification and class differences to this period. Greek and Roman civilizations are the subject of the next chapter, which tells about the ways that early intellectuals talked about food, from the austere Pythagorean regimen of barley bread and water to the Greek thinkers who founded the field of gastronomy, treating good food as a lofty expression of the human spirit. The Roman Empire built a food culture that did justice to these Greek insights, bringing together foods from all over the known world, at least for her own citizens.

The following chapter describes the food culture of the Middle Ages, a dark time in Europe and a vibrant period for the Islamic world. It was succeeded by the Renaissance, when a merchant class in Europe began to acquire wealth, expanding their global reach through trade and exploration, bringing home foods that they were able to market as status symbols. The rise of a merchant economy, with new wealth and a growing middle class, created an environment where more people could afford imported foods. European governments worked with their wealthiest citizens to colonize the lands that these foods came from, bringing in slave labor to expand their production capacity.

This led to an unprecedented global food exchange, as plants indigenous to the Americas changed the eating habits of the rest of the world. The introduction of productive, adaptable crops like potatoes and corn caused population explosions from Africa to northern Europe. This set the stage for the Industrial Revolution, when early capitalists were able to harness the abundance of labor to manufacture products that they could in turn sell to the growing pool of consumers. They learned to mass-produce products such as sugar, white flour, and even meat, foods that had lately been available mostly to the wealthy. Eating well became a commodity, an experience that almost anyone could buy. In the process, it grew cheapened. The quality of these products declined as they began to be mass-produced, and the fact that so many people could afford them made them less special.

The rest of the book explores two and a half centuries of reactions to the degraded quality of food brought to us by the mass production that started during the Industrial Revolution. From French gastronomes to Puritan preachers to modern-day Greenpeace activists and organic farmers, thinking people have looked to good food as an alternative to the ways that we have grown dehumanized by a culture that places money and efficiency ahead of kindness, health, and quality of life. The global movement for eating well has grown organically, so to speak, from our collective better instincts.

In the Beginning

ONE MORNING IN December of 1997, a paleo-anthropology graduate student fossil hunting in Ethiopia discovered an extraordinary jawbone. Yohannes Haile Selassie had a born talent for tracking old bones, and he knew right away that he'd found something special. It had larger back teeth and narrower front teeth than a modern chimpanzee, and the wear patterns on its lower canines said that it had eaten more fibrous plants and fewer leafy greens than its chimpanzee cousins.

The jawbone turned out to be roughly 5.8 million years old, dating from the time we first branched off from the simian family tree. Our brains had yet to begin shifting to their modern form, but by then our teeth and our leg bones were already changing irrevocably. Further exploration turned up foot and thigh fragments from the same period. These painted a picture of a creature starting to walk upright, improving its food gathering strategies and its diet.

Religious thinkers and scientists alike have mulled for centuries over what makes us human, debating over whether we really are all that different from other animals, especially our closest cousins, the chimpanzees and great apes. We're used to hearing about the pivotal role that our brains played in our evolution, but the decisive steps, the changes that genuinely mark our beginnings, were linked to acquiring and consuming food.

These changes in human anatomy more or less corresponded with climactic shifts in Africa, where the landscape was changing from mostly forest to a mix of trees and grassy plains. These new territories offered fresh opportunities for foraging and hunting. Compared with dense forest, the savanna provided long range views to see prey and observe other predators making kills worth scavenging. Our ancestors' recent biological changes served them well. Their upright stance let them move quickly, staying out of sight and staying out of danger.

Better foods set the stage for bigger brains, and as they grew smarter they discovered, catalogued, and transformed available foods, building on a foundation of biological and behavioral strategies time-tested by their fellow mammals. Evolutionary change favors taste buds that can discriminate between sweet foods rich in carbohydrates and bitter foods with lethal toxins. Natural selection fosters the capacity to survive tasting experiments. Individuals with digestive enzymes that can handle some potentially hazardous plant compounds are most likely to survive and pass along their genes.

Our ancestors also built on an arsenal of behavioral strategies for processing and using their food. Members of the animal kingdom regularly alter potentially edible substances to make them easier to consume and also to increase shelf life. Squirrels and primates peel fruit, and birds drop nuts from heights to crack their shells. Hyenas store food in standing water, slowing down the decay process which sets in rapidly in the African heat. As early humans began using ingenuity, tools and even fire to transform raw materials, they drew on this repertoire of techniques, improving on them in ways that were uniquely human. We can't possibly know how they felt about their food, which items they coveted, which they rejected, and which they only ate when they were desperate. Curiosity clearly played a part in their forays in search of new foods. Unlike so many other species, which are narrowly adapted to eat only a small range of plant or animal foods, humans need a wide range of nutrients, which we obtain in any number of ways. No doubt curiosity and creativity had evolutionary functions, spurring our ancestors to try new options and find new sources of necessary vitamins and minerals as their habitat changed. But in addition to the nutritional benefits, they surely experienced pleasure and excitement when they discovered new, pleasing foods or new ways of using familiar ones. Being largely migratory, they circled back around to different microclimates through revolving seasons, building taste memories of treats available at specific locations during different times of year.

Today we glorify individual celebrity chefs for their culinary accomplishments, but the indispensable foundation of our food knowledge actually comes from people whose names we will never know, the hunters and gatherers who first identified the ancestors of today's useful food plants and developed techniques for cooking, processing and storing fruits, leaves, nuts, and meats. At some point, someone discovered that the flavor of a particular root complemented the taste of a nearby leaf, birthing the art and science of building recipes. Much of this research occurred among creatures that had not yet developed larynxes capable of actual speech, although they must have had other communication strategies such as gestures and simple sounds.

The more they looked, the more variety they encountered, and over time, the quest became not simply a matter of searching and tasting but also of employing objects to expand the possibilities offered by their environment. Walking upright enabled them to use their hands for processes other than locomotion, which down the line began to include the use of tools. At first they used sticks to dig for roots and tubers, which were denser in nutrients than the leaves that their simian ancestors ate. Eventually they learned to shape stones into points that could cut and scrape carcasses. Blades and axes helped them to break through tough hides and to smash bones to get to the tasty, nutritionally dense marrow inside, an early superfood. When they ate foods that nourished them more efficiently, they grew healthier, smarter, and more energetic, qualities that in turn helped them innovate as they explored their edible landscape.

Archaeological evidence about our ancestors' diets can be misleading. Bones, or the remnants of meat consumption, tend to be better preserved than seeds, stems, and peels, the remains of a vegetable diet. Even the presence of nonhuman bones at an archaeological site does not offer crystal clear evidence that our ancestors ate these animals for dinner. Artifacts settle over millions of years. Flowing water moves objects downstream. Animal bones may indicate that our ancestors ate meat, but they could have scavenged remains from other hunting animals rather than tracking prey themselves.

Taking these factors into consideration, we have reason to believe that hominids began eating meat on a regular basis around the time that their teeth changed and they began walking upright, and it probably made up about a third of their diets. Marks on animal bones at archaeological sites suggest that protohumans did more scavenging than hunting. These grooves tell of stone tools used for the intricate work of separating meat from bones rather than striking powerful death blows. When they did hunt, their prey was mostly small animals, like birds and rodents.

They must have eaten insects as well; chimpanzees eat them, as do many indigenous tribes, and it is hard to believe they would have passed over such a readily available source of protein.

Did eating meat somehow make our ancestors smarter? Did it provide nutrition superior to what they had experienced before they learned to scavenge and hunt? Even today nutritionists and dietary experts disagree strongly among themselves about the role of meat eating in maintaining a healthy diet and whether or not it is "natural" for us to eat the flesh of other creatures. Vegetarian activists argue that eating meat on a regular basis takes its toll on our health. If we were meant to eat meat—the argument goes—we would not be developing so many diseases linked to consuming it. On the other side of the debate, some nutritionists and chefs insists that meat is inherently more satisfying and nutritionally complete than plant-based foods. Both sides use evolutionary evidence to try to prove their point. Vegetarians point to the traits that we share with herbivores–the shape of our teeth and the length of our small intestines–while proponents of meat-eating point to our ancestors' hunting skills and the uniquely human adaptations that came about when they began eating more meat.

The issue is clouded even further by the role that meat eating has played in human culture since prehistoric times. Meat has always been a special food for us. Hunting takes a level of skill, coordination, and cunning that is not required when gathering plants, although knowing the cycles and dangers of countless types of flora no doubt requires an equally substantial–though less glamorous–type of brain power. Until our ancestors began domesticating animals, the availability of meat was less predictable, and therefore more highly prized, than the supply of plant-based foods. Even once they learned to tame and breed livestock, animals were still an extravagant food source, even if we assume—for argument's sake—that the nutrients we receive from meat are superior to the ones we find in cereals and vegetables. Livestock needs to be fed, and the food they eat and the space they occupy draw down the resources available for raising crops to feed directly to humans.

Meat has almost universally been a hallmark of wealth and power. Among hunter-gatherer groups, there are highly ritualized ways of distributing the spoils of a kill. The person who fells the animal divides it ceremonially, giving the largest or most desirable organs to people of advanced age, good connections, or impressive accomplishments. Meat was used for sacrifices in early civilizations; that is, it was the food deemed most worthy of the gods. In the biblical story of Cain and Abel, God favors Abel's offering of meat over Cain's gift of vegetables.

This longstanding, universal tradition of treating meat as a special food still colors most discussions of its role in our evolution and history. But it is clear that however well or poorly we are physically adapted to eating a meat-based diet, our ancestors did hunt, scavenge, and eat animal flesh. In addition, there have been periods during our evolutionary history when increased meat consumption correlated with profound developments in technology and culture. This was the case with the emergence of the species *Homo habilis*, which lived in Africa sometime between a million and a half and two million years ago. *Habilis* is the first creature which archaeologists have bestowed with the genus name "*Homo*"; that is, he is commonly thought of as the first of our line. "*Homo habilis*" means "handy man," and this species was so named because they appear to be the first to use stone tools.

Earlier hominids probably used sticks to dig for roots, but wooden tools disintegrate so stone blades have come down to us as the earliest remnants of tool use. The tools that have been preserved from the time of *habilis* show clear signs of advancement over time, starting as crude stones that were barely altered and evolving into graceful hand axes that could only have been created with a pattern in mind. The fact that these implements were made from stone, rather than wood, suggests that they were used for dismantling animal carcasses. It takes a durable blade to break bones and puncture hides.

The increased power of reasoning which went into creating a tool and using it for a complex purpose—breaking apart an animal and handling its different parts in different ways–could easily have set the stage for the kinds of sophisticated social relationships that are unique to our species. In a community where different individuals took care of varying tasks, some must have been skilled at shaping tools, or tracking animals, or separating meat from carcasses. Others were adept at recognizing flavorful and nutritious plants and distinguishing them from poisonous species. By dividing tasks and sharing food, our ancestors were able to eat a varied and interesting diet. The cooperation necessary to make this happen could have developed into our species' unique way of sharing meals, that is, with groups extending beyond our immediate families, making eye contact and, eventually, conversation. It is probably no accident that both of these qualities–variety and conviviality–are still important aspects of what it means to eat well.

AT SOME POINT, our ancestors learned to use fire, and this knowledge changed their relationship to food and enriched their emerging culture. One common–and believable—hypothesis is that early humans tasted cooked meat when lightning strikes caused forest fires, leaving the burnt remains of creatures that had perished in the blaze. Over time they learned that they could create sparks from flint and keep flames alive by feeding them combustible materials. Now they could eat cooked foods more regularly and also stay warm and scare away predators.

There is scattered evidence of domesticated, or humanly created, fire dating from about a million and a half years ago. Evidence of early human cooking, like evidence of tool use, gives us only a general idea of how habits and technologies developed. The remnants that survive are widely scattered. Knowledge and practices appear to have begun independently in different regions and also to have spread from one place to another through travel and migration. It is clear, though, that over the hundreds of thousands of years separating *Homo habilis* and the time when anatomically human creatures began to populate most of the globe, the uses of fire became increasingly common and complex.

Fire changed our relationship with food in a variety of ways. It enhanced flavor, sealing in juices through roasting, and creating that uniquely appealing taste experience achieved through browning, or caramelization, which scientists have named the "Maillard reaction," after the French researcher who first studied it. The domestication of fire eventually led to indirect cooking techniques such as stewing and boiling. Early cooks hung animal stomachs over fires to stew, sometimes adding additional ingredients. This method enabled them to mix foods, creating complex flavors. Like modern cooks, they must have developed their own languages of combinations signifying exotic and familiar tastes.

Fire played an important part in the development of culture, or the tendency of people to come together to enjoy one another's company and use their collective skills to build something larger than they could as individuals, or even as disconnected family units. Fire provides a warm place to gather and an interesting, central phenomenon to watch. The process of cooking meals brings people together, prepping, waiting, and later enjoying the finished product. A cooked meal is a community event with different people gravitating to different tasks, from acquiring ingredients to cutting, combining, and assembling them.

Fire makes foods more digestible (although contemporary raw foods activists disagree). Some tubers, such as manioc and potatoes, are inedible in their raw states but become important staples once they are cooked. The process by which indigenous people arrived at this knowledge is mysterious and fascinating: imagine coming back to a food that has made you sick and experimenting with it until you find a less dangerous way to prepare it.

The use of fire to make food more digestible could have been instrumental in the evolution of the human brain, which, as it grew in size, required a considerable amount of energy-rich nutrients. The "expensive tissue hypothesis" was first introduced in 1995 by British anthropologists Leslie Aiello and Peter Wheeler. According to this theory, as human brains grew in size, some other organ had to grow more economical in its use of energy. Fortunately, our big brains were driving us to learn techniques for cooking and fermenting foods at the same time that they were using a disproportionate share of the nutrients we consumed. Because of these behavioral changes, we were able to get by with smaller stomachs.

Martin Jones explains:

> The so-called "expensive tissue hypothesis" proposes that possession of a big brain is plausible in energetic terms if not too strenuous a task is given to the necessarily smaller gut...Digestion is a chemical process in which large indigestible molecules are turned into

small easily absorbed molecules, and can be achieved in a variety of ways including fermentation (essentially, getting yeasts and bacteria to do the job first) and heat. The hypothesis forges a biological connection between large brain size on the one hand, and on the other, easily digestible food, or food rendered easily digestible by such processes as heat. (Jones 2007, 83-84)

We can get an idea of the brain size of early humans by measuring the bones of the cranium, but we have no way of knowing how large their guts were. We can, however, measure what remains of their teeth, and there does seem to be a correlation between growing brains and shrinking teeth and jaws, most likely because the food they ate was no longer as tough, having been softened by fire.

ANATOMICALLY MODERN HUMANS emerged between a hundred and two hundred thousand years ago in Southern Africa. Like their far-flung cousins, they subsisted initially on gathered plants and scavenged animals. Roughly 125,000 years ago, they started fishing, enjoying a diet rich in omega-6 and omega-3 fatty acids. The caves along the southern African coast hold remnants of tools far more sophisticated than those found in other parts of the world dating from the same period. Spear points are sharper and more graceful, made from stones carried from as far as a hundred miles away. It must have taken complex planning to organize journeys and haul materials. There could even have been trade occurring with neighbors who lived closest to the best sources of flint.

Hunting activity dramatically accelerated in this part of the world around seventy thousand years ago. This dating is

significant because it roughly corresponds with the most p
erful volcanic eruption on record: Mt. Toba, on the island we
now know as Sumatra. This dramatic geological event affected climate all over the globe, triggering an especially severe ice
age and leading to the extinction of countless species. Our ancestors were forced to innovate and become more resourceful in
their quest for food.

During the years following this catastrophic eruption, the sophisticated tool-making technologies that had previously been
found only in the southern part of Africa began spreading, following a northbound route. Climatic changes forced these
communities to move far afield in search of more hospitable
places to live. They traveled through the northern part of Africa
then through the Middle East and eventually into Europe over
the course of about twenty-five thousand years.

There is evidence that anatomically modern humans had
reached the Middle East long before this, where they shared
the region with Neanderthal populations. But the *Homo sapiens* who reached Israel and Syria as early as a hundred thousand
years earlier had not brought the cultural innovations that came
with this later wave, the finely shaped tools and body decora-
tions which could only have been products of an advanced social
system. The earlier arrivals resembled modern humans physically, but their cultural developments–or lack of them–belonged
to an earlier era.

As the newcomers spread into Europe between forty and
fifty thousand years ago, the Neanderthal populations that had
lived there for hundreds of thousands of years quickly died
out. Perhaps there was direct confrontation, but it is also likely
that the Neanderthals just couldn't compete for resources. The
modern *Homo sapiens* were faster on their feet, and they were

weapons that they could throw from a dis-
the amount of space separating them from
unters considerably improved their odds of
uld escape more quickly when their efforts
w. l, and they could more easily stalk prey without
alerting them .. the imminent threat.

Big game hunting became a day-to-day survival strategy requiring careful coordination among groups searching for prey.
Hunters learned the movements and habits of a range of species, developing systems for stalking herds, isolating vulnerable
individuals, and calling the best moment to strike. They used
fire to transform habitat, driving animals towards their ready
spears, and they planned chases to channel herds into dead
ends or over cliffs.

They clearly used some kind of speech to convey their ideas
and intentions. Even our simian cousins communicate with
grunts and gestures, so it is safe to assume that the process of lin-
guistically conveying meaning and information evolved over a
considerable time. Obviously, there is no archaeological evidence
of speech per se, but by the time these anatomically human, culturally sophisticated hunters began moving north from southern
Africa, they had developed a larynx capable of producing the
sounds found in modern languages. Beyond that, we can speculate about the beginnings of spoken language from evidence
of behaviors and accomplishments that would have been virtually impossible without the complex communication that
speech facilitates.

Interpersonal bonds grew richer and family ties grew stronger as individuals conveyed needs and nuances of feeling.
Community members understood complex social relationships,
learning about roles and relationships in practical and symbolic

terms. This changed their relationship with food, adding meaning to the act of sharing. Like today, eating was a way to bring people together, to celebrate a windfall or to make sure everyone had enough when resources were scarce. But it was also a way to establish and reinforce hierarchy, with powerful or older individuals eating first or helping themselves to the best portions.

Human hunting transformed the landscape. The big game that were their targets, the European hippopotamus, wooly rhinoceros, bison, red deer, and wooly mammoths, had to adapt quickly to a new–and lethal—predator. Some were hunted to extinction, in fact, there is a strong correlation between human migration to other continents—especially Australia and North and South America—and the disappearance of the large mammals that had ruled the landscape.

In Africa and to some extent in Europe, big game species gradually adjusted to the threat, adapting by learning fear and growing quicker. The sudden mass extinctions that occurred in the rest of the world weren't nearly as dramatic on those continents. But where modern humans descended on an area with tools, language, and knowledge that were already advanced enough to do damage, many indigenous species couldn't compete.

The sudden windfall was surely exciting for the hunters. Meat, which had previously made up only a small part of their diets, became an everyday staple. They grew arrogant, taking more than they needed. Perhaps they also binged as a way to cope with the uncertainties they faced daily, the harsh climate and the shifting landscape. Ice age humans lived in an era of scarcity and bounty, fighting for survival and coming through by virtue of their resourcefulness and ingenuity.

They lived reasonably well despite the hardships. Many important innovations date from this time when our ancestors began building shelters, sewing clothing, and making art. At first they covered themselves with furs, and then they learned to weave, creating nets for fishing, sacks for holding gathered plant foods, and adornments for their bodies. They learned to fire clay. At first they did not use this important technology to make practical objects like bowls, pots, and water jugs. Instead, they made earthenware sculptures, animal shapes, and the famous "fertility goddesses" portraying opulent female figures.

They created the exquisite cave paintings in the south of France which still move us today. These scenes show human figures flinging spears at herds of different animal species. Other cave walls depict creatures with some human and some animal features. Although their exact meaning is lost, we are left with the obvious fact that they are meaningful. Someone took the trouble of crawling long distances through dark, tight spaces and then creating these paintings with precision and care. Some of the caves were visited over a period of ten thousand years, indicating a continuous tradition of complex rituals. Similar figures appear in far-flung caves, hinting that distant communities shared myths and stories.

The shamanic figures showing creatures that were part human and part animal tell us that these hunters identified on some level with their hunting victims. Humans, too, had a history of serving as prey, especially for large cat species. They had mythologies explaining the passage from life to death. They buried their dead, sometimes with adornments and provisions, and they also grappled with the deaths they inflicted on the animals they hunted. Their search for food had grown undeniably spiritual, as they linked their physical quest for nourishment with a longing for broader meaning. Eating became more than just eating; it also involved forging relationships and taking lives.

This spirituality did not emerge fully blown at this late stage in our evolutionary development. Joseph Campbell describes configurations unearthed at Neanderthal sites:

> In Drachenloch and Wildermannlisloch little walls of stone, up to 32 inches high, formed a kind of bin, within which a number of cave-bear skulls had been carefully arranged. Some of these skulls had little stones arranged around them; others were set on slabs; one, very carefully placed, had the long bones of a cave bear (no doubt its own) placed beneath its snout; another had the long bones pushed through the orbits of its eyes. (Campbell 1959, 341)

Paleolithic cave art created a place for people to congregate and share rituals. These gatherings probably included music.

> The French archaeologists Iegor Reznikoff and Michel Dauvois conducted detailed surveys of three decorated caves in the Ariege region of southwest France. Unconventionally, they were not looking for stone tools, engraved objects, or new paintings. They were singing. More specifically, they moved slowly through the caves, stopping repeatedly to test the resonance of each section. Using notes spanning three octaves, they drew up a resonance map of each cave and discovered that those areas with highest resonance were also those most likely to harbor a painting or engraving. (Leakey 1994, 111)

By about thirty-five thousand years ago, Europe was deep in an especially severe glacial period. Polar ice sheets covered most of

Europe leaving only a few habitable areas, including the south of France where the greatest density of cave art occurs. Competition among hunters for game grew fierce. By fifteen to twenty thousand years ago, an especially rich period for cave art, some of the larger mammals were beginning to disappear even in the more temperate parts of Europe.

To make up for the gap in their diet caused by the growing shortfall of meat, humans turned back to the plant world which had long sustained them. The last major ice age finally drew to a close, and the polar ice sheets receded from much of Europe, leaving a landscape teeming with edible wild plants, especially the large seeded grasses native to the Fertile Crescent in southwestern Asia, the area covering much of present day Turkey, Syria, and Iraq.

Residents of this area learned to cultivate the grains they harvested, selecting and planting the most useful seeds. Like the European hunters before them, they changed their diets by innovating. In the process, they also transformed their landscape, forging a new balance with their plant and animal neighbors. Their culture morphed as their days took on a different rhythm and their routines grew more sedentary.

For better or for worse, at the end of the last major ice age, we started down the road to becoming farmers.

Seeds of Civilization

ACCORDING TO POLYNESIAN myth, the great eel monster's lover took a new beau. The eel monster fought his rival, who killed the great monster and buried his body. A coconut tree grew out of his remains, and that is the origin of the coconut. Another version of the tale uses breadfruit instead.

There are similar stories all over the world, even in the Americas. The Obijway tribe tells of a boy on a solitary retreat, a rite of passage into manhood. A stranger from the sky visited daily. They wrestled, but the boy was weak from fasting. The visitor encouraged him, and on the final day, the boy killed the celestial guest, buried his body, and tended and weeded the spot until late summer when he found a stalk of corn growing there. This is how corn came into the world.

These myths are ancient. If they come from a single tale, it dates back even before humans reached the Americas. Each version associates violence with the act of growing food. Similarly, farming links to sorrow in the biblical Eden story. When God expels Adam and Eve from the garden for disobeying God's injunction against eating from the Tree of Life, their descendants must feed themselves "by the sweat of (their) brow," that is, through the repetitive, hard labor of farming. Agriculture is a punishment. Adam and Eve can no longer live easily in the garden, plucking ripe fruit from God's perfect trees.

History books tell of the great achievements of early agricultural settlements, who invented writing, functional pottery, and architecture. But these developments took thousands of years. It was not apparent to the first farmers that their new technologies would create so many opportunities for coming generations. The myths from that time instead express the loss of something comfortable and familiar.

We think of the lives of hunters and gatherers as precarious and unpredictable, but humans seem to have lived quite well this way, at least in most parts of the globe. Current and ancient wisdom says that it is best for us to eat a wide variety of foods, and hunter-gatherers enjoyed hundreds of options while only the most adventurous agriculturalists grow more than a few dozen. Studies of fossilized skeletons from all over the world show a surge in diseases caused by nutritional deficiencies starting around the time people stopped hunting and gathering and began farming. They worked harder as well. Contemporary hunter-gatherers devote only about four hours a day to the labor of finding food, but agriculture involves long hours and heavy lifting. The bones of early farmers show signs of the type of wear and tear caused by ongoing, repetitive toil.

Why did our ancestors leave behind a livelihood that nourished them well in favor of a backbreaking workload providing inferior food? They started farming because they could; because for the first time in nearly a hundred thousand years, the climate was stable enough for them to predict the life cycles of plants. The ice ages, in addition to being cold, had been a time of dramatic temperature swings, even over the course of a few years. Our ancestors also started farming because they had to, because the abundance of food available in the warmer weather swelled their numbers until they passed the land's capacity to feed themselves on wild foods alone. Hunting also grew challenging as some big mammal species grew extinct while others moved north, following their receding icy habitat.

Nobody sat down, weighed their options, and chose agriculture; yet the transition was swift and in some way inevitable. The technology developed independently in at least three different regions and then spread to most parts of the globe in six or eight thousand years, a remarkable speed when you consider the fact that other innovations, like tools and fire, took up to a million years to catch on. Almost every culture on the planet eventually adopted some form of agriculture and animal husbandry.

The earliest agricultural activity uncovered to date began in the area known as the "Fertile Crescent" in southwestern Asia, where large seeded grasses—the ancestors of today's wheat, rye, and barley—grew wild. The area that we now know as the Middle East did not experience the kind of severe ice age that had occurred in northern Europe, but it did benefit from the gradual warming which began to occur about fifteen thousand years ago. Its climate grew wetter, more hospitable to plants. In some areas, edible plants grew so abundantly that hunter gatherers could camp for most of the year near fields of wild grain, harvesting as needed. The most successful of these settlements were situated along migration routes for gazelle, their favorite source of meat.

Among the early wild varieties of wheat, most had fragile husks which shattered easily, allowing the plant to reseed itself. Natural genetic diversity also hatched individual plants with hulls that did not shatter, and the people who gathered them found this variation useful: the un-hulled grain did not need to be eaten right away. It could be stored and husked as needed. The predecessors of the first farmers saved seeds from the storable wheat and scattered them in the wild fields, increasing the proportion of useful plants. Full-fledged agriculture was still thousands of years in the future, but plant genetics thirteen thousand years ago were already being changed by human tinkering.

These innovators managed gazelle populations as well. Carole Cope, a researcher at Hebrew University in Jerusalem, studied bones found at two ancient sites dated several hundred years apart. Remains from feasts dating to the earlier period showed roughly equal numbers of male and female animals, indicating that hunters had at first been indiscriminate, taking prey of both sexes. But the bones from the later site were disproportionately male: humans were managing the herds, leaving females alive to reproduce.

The period of sedentary hunter-gatherers just before the Neolithic Age was a good time to live in the Near East. These cultures—known as Natufians— had the stability that later communities earned through the labor of farming without the hard work of tilling the soil. Food was so abundant that they did not need to wander. They knew where they were going to sleep and what they were going to eat. They had sophisticated customs, which included traditions and conventions for handling different foods.

At one site on the shores of Lake Kinneret (the Sea of Galilee) in Israel, different categories of edibles were stored in separate huts. Fish were kept apart from birds, and seeds gathered from different shores had dedicated bins. There are no remnants of fish scales, and mammal bones also appear to have been butchered someplace else. Some tasks belonged within the boundaries of the community, and others did not. Flora and fauna came with beliefs and stories, and food had spiritual weight.

This way of life drew to a close around 10,800 BC with the onset of a twelve-hundred-year cold spell. It was brief compared to the ice ages which had just passed, but it was long enough to destroy the Natufian culture. They deserted their settlements, forced to travel further afield in search of food. They brought their seeds with them, along with their knowledge of how to tend plants. When the warm weather returned around 9600 BC, their descendants were ready to farm.

Agriculture became a deliberate act. The first farmers transformed their landscape, and it changed them as well. Hunter-gatherer mythologies had been built around finding a place in the wild landscape, learning the habits and habitats of creatures and plants. Neolithic—or early farming—cultural artifacts tell instead of a people fascinated by their newfound ability to mold their world. Their lives became predictable, with rhythms and routines. The people—as well as their plants and animals— became domesticated, living apart from nature, in houses.

Early Near Eastern families buried their dead beneath the floorboards of their dwellings, maintaining continuity between generations and rooting residents to their homes. With the beginnings of agriculture, people began building rectangular structures instead of round ones. Families could add rooms logically and geometrically, and they could subdivide, designating separate spaces for sleeping, cooking, eating, or praying. CatalHoyok, in eastern Turkey—one of the largest Neolithic sites ever found—was situated close to the best sources of plaster, though the fields its residents tended were seven miles away. They chose to live near their building materials rather than with their work and their food.

They fired and decorated pottery. Artisans wove fabrics and shaped beads from bones, stones, and even metal. Their sedentary days enabled them to design and store cooking equipment, acquiring tools and technologies for creating useful foods and interesting meals. They made flour from wheat and rye, which they shaped into flat breads to cook on stones. Later they invented clay ovens. They learned the art of fermentation to make bread and beer. As they grew innovative with yeasts and doughs, they selected seeds from more glutinous varieties of wheat, those that made the best bread. Their plants continued to grow domesticated, further removed from nature.

They celebrated the wild as well as the tame, fascinated by the relationship between the two, which was evolving in front of their eyes. Excavators at CatalHoyok unearthed a figure that was clearly female, with breasts and a swollen abdomen, and a seed from a cereal grain buried in the exact center of her back. The precise location of the seed indicated that it was placed there intentionally, and laboratory analysis revealed that it came from a wild grain rather than a domesticated one.

A good deal has been written about the so-called "fertility cults" of the Near East, dating from around this time, harkening back to much older figures from parts of Europe and the Near East. These sculptures are archetypally female, with pendulous breasts, pregnant bellies, and, for the most part, truncated feet. James Mellaart, the original excavator at Catalhoyok, interpreted them as evidence of an ancient goddess religion. He wrote around the time that the Women's Movement was coming into its own, and feminist writers made much of these finds, using them to show that patriarchy was neither inevitable nor necessary.

The evidence that has accumulated over time has made the issue murkier rather than clearer. Many of the artifacts that were originally identified as female have shown, on closer examination, to have no clear gender. Others are unquestionably female, and they clearly played some role in the spiritual and mythological life of the people of CatalHoyok, part of a culture and belief system which they shared with other communities in the area. The idea of fertility understandably captured their imagination: it was the mechanism by which food was abundant rather than scarce. It was a natural phenomenon, one that occurred outside of their sphere of influence, yet they were learning how to exert some measure of control over it by breeding animals as well as plants.

Sheep and goats were the first domesticated food animals in the Near East, where herdsmen began tending them several thousand years after farming began in earnest. The size of animal bones offers a clue to chronology: domesticated strains tend to be smaller than wild ones. At first herders continued taking wild prey while also feeding and raising animals of their own, but over time domesticated animals became their main source of meat.

Like farming, the domestication of food animals evolved independently in different parts of the world. Dogs had already been living symbiotically with humans for tens of thousands of years, and cats became human companions during early Neolithic times. Both dogs and cats probably domesticated themselves by venturing close to human camps, where they enjoyed the warmth of the fires and the bounty of food scraps. Over time their skills proved useful, with cats keeping a lid on rodent populations and dogs providing companionship, early warnings about intruders, and hunting prowess. Pigs were domesticated early in the Far East, where they could have joined human populations in a fashion similar to dogs and cats, drawn to surplus food. They must have been a nuisance at first until it became apparent that they kept human homesteads cleaner, removing waste that could have attracted more dangerous predators.

Like plants, domesticated animals changed genetically through their contact with humans. Tameness, or the ability to live in confinement with other creatures, is not just a personality trait but also a function of low adrenal output, a limited supply of the chemical that produces the "fight or flight" response. This hormone is useful in the wild, where animals need to be on guard for predators and prey, but it is an inconvenient trait in livestock. Animals with high adrenal output reproduce poorly in captivity, so the process of domestication automatically selects for tamer animals.

Like agriculture, animal husbandry makes little sense for communities with ample supplies of wild foods. Why feed precious grains to sheep and goats when self-sufficient animals roam nearby for easy hunting? Livestock provide dairy products and help to till the fields, but their many secondary uses weren't immediately obvious to the people who first domesticated them. It took thousands of years for farmers to discover that they could culture their animals' milk to make cheese and yogurt. The first domesticated sheep had long, stiff hair that wasn't useful for spinning wool. The people who first tamed aurochs, the ancestors of today's cows, had no idea that they would be able to hitch these animals to plows.

Perhaps the domestication of livestock did not begin for practical reasons at all. Virtually all hunter-gatherer cultures had myths and rituals expressing kinship with the animal world and sanctifying the act of hunting. Hunters were powerful people. They shared the meat they brought, garnering respect and homage. Long established links between meat, power, and sacredness carried over into the Neolithic practice of animal sacrifice. Whoever corralled and fed the wild creatures that became the first tame livestock was sufficiently well off to feed them spare grain. Like his ancestors who felled wild beasts, he earned prestige through his capacity to distribute meat, and the balance of power in his community shifted in his favor, setting the stage for the more advanced forms of social stratification which characterized later ancient civilizations.

The bones of ancient livestock often turn up among the remains of feasts, meals that were prepared in special vessels and included quantities of food no family could possibly have eaten on a daily basis. Killing and eating livestock was a way to celebrate important events like births and weddings. At some point, butchering also became an occasion in itself: someone could decide to slaughter a couple of sheep or goats simply in order to show off and curry favor with their neighbors or create the perception that he had a special relationship with the gods.

People of the Neolithic Near East feasted on wild animals as well as tame ones. Each had its own significance in the mythological life of the community. At Catalhoyok, many homes had bulls' horns mounted on the walls, and paintings made lavish use of bull imagery. Being used to domesticated cattle, it is difficult for us to imagine the huge wild bulls of that era. Apart from their considerable size, they were ornery and aggressive, nothing like the docile cows that graze in modern pastures. Perhaps they were so central to the community's iconography because they represented the staggering power of nature, a force to be reckoned with in spite of recent human achievements.

In other parts of the world as well, people celebrated the wild also even as their lives grew sedentary and domesticated. At a site in southern England known as Hambledon Hill, archaeologists have uncovered remains of feasts that occurred over thousands of years. The artifacts contain traces of domesticated wheat and barley as well as tame sheep, goats, and even cattle, in addition to the remnants of wild plants and animals. These revelers lived mostly around forested areas and probably grew grains on the outskirts of woods. This was not the kind of concentrated, intensive endeavor that would have left a recognizable imprint on the landscape. Rather, their farming was part of a mostly nomadic existence, which over time had integrated some elements of the "Neolithic package."

Agricultural knowledge had spread through the region as farmers from the Near East migrated over centuries and millennia in search of fertile lands. The relatively predictable food supply they had learned to produce through agricultural technologies swelled their numbers until they outgrew their former homelands. In addition, early farming communities had not yet learned the art of restoring nutrients to the soil by composting and fertilizing, so their plots grew increasingly less productive until they had to move on in search of more fertile ground. As the newcomers settled, the indigenous people they met adopted some of their technologies. Immigrants and natives married. Geneticists studying the DNA of contemporary Europeans tentatively conclude that, on average, about twenty percent of their genetic material comes from Neolithic Near Eastern immigrants to the area, while eighty percent comes from Europeans whose roots can be traced back to the ice ages. The science is relatively new and hardly conclusive, but it is fascinating.

The people who feasted at Hambledon Hill in southern England had clearly been influenced by the cultural and agricultural innovations that started in the Near East more than five thousand years earlier. They also had firmly established local traditions, belonging to a network of communities that were related to one another, having occupied the same landscape for many generations. Neighboring tribes marked their identities relative to one another by bringing different traditional foods to their feasts, showing off regional variations. Their distinctive clothing and songs proclaimed each group's individuality. Yet, for all their differences, they still shared a common culture.

There are no remains of fish at the site, despite abundant water nearby. People throughout the British Isles had eaten plenty of fish since their earliest days in the area. The conspicuous absence of fish remnants suggests that this community must have shunned fish deliberately, probably because of a taboo. It may have represented a wilder, more primitive way of life, a subsistence food that they had transcended. Like the inhabitants of the settlement at Lake Kinneret who cleaned the meat and fish outside of the boundaries of their community, the foods that were eaten by these ancient inhabitants of the British Isles were more than just nutrients put into their bodies to sustain life. They also served symbolic and mythological purposes, expressing beliefs and assumptions about right and wrong ways to live, linking them to some neighbors and separating them from others.

PERHAPS THE BEST-KNOWN food taboo in the modern world, the Jewish and Muslim injunction against eating pigs, began during the Neolithic period. We hear many explanations for this prohibition, ranging from the dangers of trichinosis to the fact that the pig was deified by some early Near Eastern civilizations. The act of shunning it could have been a way for the new monotheistic religions to set themselves apart from their neighbors. But the avoidance of pig meat in the Middle East reaches back long before the origins of Judaism and Islam.

By about 2400 BC, a wide range of Middle Eastern cultures had taboos in place forbidding the consumption of pork products. Climatic changes taking place in the area around that time made the landscape drier and less wooded. Pigs thrive in forested landscapes, where they feed on tubers, roots, and nuts. Unlike cows that can digest the cellulose rich grasses which humans don't eat, pigs eat a similar diet to humans when their natural woodland habitat is not available. In wooded areas, they do not compete with humans for food, but in drier, grassier areas, they do, making them an inefficient source of meat in the ancient Near East.

This taboo evolved gradually. It addressed a practical issue, yet it spread as a divine injunction. Similarly, the prohibition against eating cows and the widespread vegetarianism on the Indian subcontinent appeared early and could very well be a collective solution to an environmental food crisis, couched in religious terms. The density of the area's population made it impractical for everyone to consume meat on a daily basis, so religious texts threatened dire spiritual consequences for anyone who ate it. Despite their practical origins, these taboos against eating cows and pigs, and meat in general, were more than just food distribution strategies. They were sacred, meaningful ways for people to rise above themselves.

Although food scarcities sometimes led to restrictions and taboos, they often had exactly the opposite effect. Rare commodities became status symbols and treats for special occasions. The first domesticated livestock, which consumed precious food stocks, were symbols of wealth and prestige. As Neolithic times were succeeded by the Bronze Age, pronounced divisions developed between people who could afford to eat lavishly and others who ate more monotonous, less nutritious diets.

During the Bronze Age, deeply stratified societies developed in parts of the Middle East and South Asia. These social developments corresponded with demographic changes, as Indo-Europeans from the northern Eurasian steppes migrated into the area, bringing new myths and customs. Much of our knowledge about their migrations comes from their momentous impact on European, southwest Asian, and Indian languages. In fact, because of the colonialism of recent history, today the majority of the world's nations speak languages with Indo-European roots.

Indo-European culture probably came into its own roughly five or six thousand years ago and began spreading southwards and westwards by about 2500 BC. By the time the Indo-Europeans began migrating, they had already adopted many elements of the Neolithic revolution. They practiced some agriculture but not as intensively as communities further south. They distinguished themselves as stock breeders, a livelihood well suited to their grassy homeland.

They were the first to domesticate the horse, and this development had a dramatic impact on their culture and history, and also on the evolution of the rest of the world. The use of horses for transportation made the Indo-Europeans more mobile than any other civilization had been to date. It enabled them to cover a substantial area in search of pastureland, and it facilitated their migrations to other parts of the late Neolithic world. It also gave them a military edge over virtually everyone in their path.

The grazing herds of these Indo-European warriors steadily depleted the nutrients in available pastures, forcing them to perpetually wander farther afield. Migrations took place over about two thousand years. As they settled in different lands, they adopted many of their new neighbors' technologies and customs. Cultures also mixed through trade and intermarriage. The

Indo-Europeans who moved westward and southward as part of later migrations met the descendants of former neighbors who had settled the area during previous waves, people who had already become strangers.

Their pottery and burial mounds had distinctive regional and cultural styles, enabling modern archaeologists to trace their expansions. The development and spread of languages also offers information about the mixing of newcomers with longtime inhabitants of the lands where they settled. These clues come from written records created hundreds and even thousands of years after the Indo-Europeans first arrived. Despite the periods of time that separate these writings from the early migrations, researchers have managed to untangle useful clues by comparing words and names across regions and evaluating the results relative to the emergence of cultural, agricultural, and technological developments.

The Indo-European class structure that linguists have been able to reconstruct relied on a clear social hierarchy, dividing citizens into priests, warriors, and herder-agriculturalists. Priests and warriors ranked higher than food producers. Indo-European mythology also made frequent reference to twins, which symbolize separation between two halves of a whole. Their art, customs, and rituals expressed divisions between the sexes more markedly than artifacts from other cultures dating from the same time.

Under the influence of these myths and customs, late Neolithic and early Bronze Age civilizations became less peaceful and more differentiated, emphasizing separations between their own and neighboring cultures and also between different classes and genders within their own communities. Feminist thinkers from Marija Gimbutas to Mary Daly have argued that this development came about as a result of unequal military confrontations where peaceful natives were no match for the warlike intruders, but the situation was more complex than a simple clash of opposing forces.

Indo-Europeans mythology and culture arrived in a world that was ripe for social stratification. Thousands of years of farming had spawned technologies such as plowing and irrigation which increased efficiency and created surpluses. Shrewd strategists acquired more than they needed, gaining an edge over their neighbors. Enterprising craftsmen created secondary products such as bread, milk, cheese, and wool. Talented workmen acquired valuable skills, building wealth through commerce and trade. Inequities accumulated, and war became an institution, even a way of life.

Despite the escalating violence, this was not simply a period of aggression and conflict. Visionary thinkers openly criticized the widespread violence and greed. An Iranian prophet named Zoroaster spoke of opposing forces of good and evil struggling to rule the world. He mythologized this fight as a struggle between cattle and wolves, echoing the metaphors for domestication and wildness, which, as we have seen, figured prominently in the mythology of earlier Neolithic cultures. By Zoroaster's day, they also represented the newer conflict between the mostly peaceful ways of the early agricultural communities and the warlike, stratified societies which were emerging.

By speaking out against the violence he saw all around him, Zoroaster set the stage for a new kind of religion and spirituality that would emerge during the upcoming period, one which valued human compassion and kindness over currying favor with the gods. He may have been the first thinker to define good and evil as abstract qualities, rather than traits embodied by specific deities.

Many of the teachers who later followed in Zoroaster's foot-steps, from Pythagoras to Mani, linked the physical world with evil and the spiritual world with good. This ideological split between the body and the soul had important consequences for our relationship with food: if the body is merely an inconvenient vessel, then food should be just a matter of subsistence, or staying alive. Culinary pleasure and variety were distractions from the real work of nourishing the soul.

The new ideas circulating at the beginning of the Iron Age grew out of a complex world with strangers living side by side, witnessing and adopting each other's customs, languages, technologies, and foods. The emerging societies were diversified enough to support priestly and warrior castes as well as artisans and craftsmen. Eventually, cooks and bakers joined the ranks of specialized professionals, perfecting their art and writing recipes, creating a canon.

Granaries of the Gods

I GREW UP IN Brooklyn, and when I first moved to the West Coast, I often asked East Coast visitors to bring me bagels. Similarly, many ancient Babylonian tablets bear messages exchanged among friends, relatives, and travelers requesting special meats, cakes, and fruits. Other correspondence praises or complains about the quality or frequency of these shipments.

> Good health, my brother! You know that for some time, you haven't been sending me garlic, onions, or *sirbittu* fish... (Bottero 2004, 18)

These Babylonian tablets also contain the earliest known written recipes:

> **Salted Broth**. Leg of mutton, but no (other) meat is used. Prepare water; add fat; dodder as desired; salt to taste; cypress; onion, *samidu*; cumin; coriander; leek and garlic, mashed with *kisimmu*. It is ready to serve. (Bottero 2004, 28)

41

THESE INSTRUCTIONS FOR preparing salted broth were part of a collection offering directions for basics including soup, meat, and vegetables. Unlike modern cookbooks, which specify exact cooking times and sizes and shapes for prepping ingredients, these recipes assume a degree of knowledge. Even quantities are vague: presumably the experienced cook knew how much to use, just as he knew how to "prepare water." These tablets offer insight into a highly developed cuisine with established conventions and variations on themes. They tell us that, by this point in Mesopotamian history, cooking had grown into a courtly art practiced by professionals. Guidelines are set down in writing: professional cooks belonged to the class of people who could read.

The English sociologist Jack Goody studied the question of why some cultures have an haute cuisine—a difference in complexity separating the diets of the rich and the poor—rather than simply a difference in quantity, with rich people eating more and poor people eating less of a core group of staple foods. He concluded that literacy makes the difference, allowing cooks and chroniclers to document techniques and recipes for future generations. Under the influence of these early Mesopotamian cooks and scribes, culinary knowledge began evolving from an oral tradition into an expansive body of written work.

Mesopotamian civilization was the first to produce enough grain to feed an infrastructure of bureaucrats. Taxmen in ancient Mesopotamia collected grain, beer, and animals to provision temples and government institutions, and they kept careful inventories. The very earliest written tablets tracked accounts of food stocks. Merchants used written notations as well, recording products shipped and received.

Mesopotamia's economy quickly came to be organized from above by a government actively involved in public works, religious ceremonies, and construction projects. The geography of the land was uniquely suited to these developments, though the ingenuity of the people cannot be underestimated. Ancient Mesopotamia lay between two mighty rivers. Water was abundant, but rain was scarce. The teeming rivers periodically flooded their banks, covering the soil with water saturated with minerals. These trace elements continued to nourish the soil long after the moisture evaporated.

It was an environment with vast potential which could only be realized if people worked together to harness the rivers' potential. They rose to the challenge and learned to irrigate, building canals to channel the water in the direction of lands off the main course of the river. When flooding changed the contours of the landscape, they came together again and rebuilt, adapting to new conditions.

At first this was a grassroots effort with neighbors lending each other a hand. Over time farmers who had settled on the most auspiciously positioned lands began producing more grain than they needed. They saw the possibilities that the landscape offered, the vast increases in productivity which could occur if irrigation were practiced on a wider scale. This required a considerable labor force, harnessing the efforts of individuals with leadership skills and engineering acumen.

Leaders initially cast themselves as gods incarnate and later as the agents of the gods. They traded some of their rapidly accumulating surplus for the materials to build temples, where they stored grain to redistribute to workers who toiled to create additional public works. According to an ancient Babylonian myth, there were originally two classes of gods: those who governed but did not work and, beneath them, those who labored to meet the community's daily needs. When the working gods grew dissatisfied and went on strike, the ruling gods created man out of clay to labor at the chores the lower gods had shunned. Human society mirrored the divine world with leaders who ruled and workers who toiled. The striking laborer gods had been replaced and made obsolete; this widely known tale warned that a similar fate lay in store for human workers who contemplated rebellion.

Unlike the incorporeal god of the Hebrew Bible, the Babylonian gods needed to eat. Temple archives list copious quantities of food required by the gods as well as specifications detailing how it should be prepared. These provisions were supplied on a daily basis with special requirements for feasts falling on designated days of the calendar year. Temples maintained a culinary infrastructure dedicated to fashioning foods: butchers who slaughtered livestock, cooks who roasted fish and fowl, and millers and bakers who ground grain and baked flatbreads. The food probably went to feed priests and temple workers, who also sold leftovers to pay for temple maintenance. On feasts and holidays, they invited a wider audience to dine.

The organizational structure, which created the productive Mesopotamian irrigation works, also built an effective war machine. Within the specialized economy, craftsmen excelled at different trades. A class of skilled metalsmiths produced tools and weapons from copper, then bronze–an alloy of copper and tin–and eventually iron. Armies defended territory from outsiders who were drawn to the civilization's abundance. Leaders grew eager to multiply the success of local organizing by controlling larger areas. Neighboring city-states feuded.

The great cultural developments of early Mesopotamian civilization started in the south, among an ethnic group known as the Sumerians. By the later part of the third millennium BC, a northern Iraqi Semitic people called the Akkadians gained the upper hand in the ongoing territorial disputes. The Akkadians had been nomadic herders until they settled down and adopted many of the agricultural practices that the Sumerians had instituted so successfully. Their nomadic background gave them a military edge: pastoral cultures tend to be more aggressive than agriculturalists because their wanderings bring them into regular conflict with strangers. The Akkadians believed in a pantheon of gods and were not as reverent as the southerners who, as farmers, needed to appease the forces regulating the well-being of their crops: the sun, the wind, and the water.

Under Akkadian rule, land became a commodity that could be privately owned. At first individuals earned titles to plots when they performed exemplary military service or were otherwise useful to the state, and some families claimed ownership simply by virtue of having settled on a parcel first. It wasn't long before all the arable land had been claimed either by the state, the temples, or individual landholding families.

Neighbors who did not own land exchanged their labor for wages, or they leased plots in order to grow their own crops. The class of landless workers expanded as the region grew more densely populated over succeeding generations. Families who had originally owned land but fell on hard times sold it unwillingly. Existing landowners increased the size of their estates. Social and economic distance widened between property owners and their tenants. The wealth and power which had once belonged exclusively to priests and kings now graced landowners as well. Agricultural workers found it difficult to prosper. Not only did they have to pay a share of their harvest to lease their fields, but land owners and grain merchants could take advantage of their misfortunes by manipulating prices and raising rents.

Out of this unjust situation, the beginnings of a justice system emerged. We know about ancient Babylonian law largely from the Code of Hammurabi, a list of regulations inscribed on basalt tablets during the second millennium BC. Early in the twentieth century AD, French archaeologists unearthed these stone documents in southwestern Iran, where they had probably landed as war trophies.

Babylonian law had little to do with the gods or with any abstract idea of morality. Its purpose was to maintain order and prosperity. Agricultural workers needed enough to eat so they could grow food for others. Hammurabi's code specifies standard wages for different types of work. Like today's minimum wage laws, these statutes protected the workers by ensuring that they would not earn less, but they also helped employers who had legal ground to pay no more than the statute required. Likewise, the rules governing rental of fields protected both owners and tenants. A tenant farmer could keep one-third of what he produced, but he had to pay the remaining two-thirds to the land owner. Workers were guaranteed a share of the harvest, but it was a smaller amount than they paid to the landlords, who did none of the work.

Mesopotamian society came into its own by virtue of unprecedented agricultural expertise and inventiveness. But as its political and economic systems developed, the people who worked the soil assumed the lowest place in the social hierarchy. Grain was currency, the foundation of the economy, but one could earn considerably more respect by counting it or trading it than by growing it.

A strong merchant class emerged as political power shifted from the Sumerians in the south to the Akkadians in the north. The land was poor in trees, metal, and stone. Materials for durable buildings, plows, and weapons had to be acquired from abroad. Traders exchanged grain for luxury items such as precious stones, especially lapis lazuli, and aromatics such as frankincense and myrrh. They traded for spices as well, maintaining trading networks with communities as distant as the Harrappan civilization in the Indus Valley, a source of cardamom. They imported spices in order to season their food, but these flavorings took on broader meaning, serving as emblems of wealth and taste. These seasonings from distant lands altered the taste of food but added little nutritional value. They were expensive and exotic, available only to those with resources to spare.

Mesopotamian merchants also traded for spices from Egypt, another highly advanced Middle Eastern civilization. The secrets of ancient Egypt have offered themselves up to modern researchers more readily than those of Mesopotamia. The Egyptians built in stone, rather than brick, so more of their structures survive. Their famous pyramid tombs provide a wealth of information about the daily lives of ordinary people, in contrast to the Akkadian tablets, which mostly documented courtly activities.

The ancient Egyptians believed in an afterlife which mirrored the present world. They left provisions of food for the deceased to eat once they awakened in the other realm. Paintings and writings on the walls of tombs provide instructions for basic tasks, as well as illustrations of daily activities and industries such as bread production. The mummified remains of human bodies also provide information about their diets.

Like Mesopotamia, Egypt has a unique geography which was instrumental to its development as a civilization. Its landscape was similarly centered on the flow of a river which periodically overflowed, watering an otherwise arid land and bringing valuable nutrients to the soil. The Nile River flooded at predictable intervals, unlike the Tigris and Euphrates, which were more whimsical.

Early Egyptian astronomers learned to track the seasons and the movements of the stars accurately enough to predict the river's schedule. This knowledge made them powerful, and they did not readily share it. Perhaps they claimed that they controlled these events or that they interceded with the deities who caused them. Their information about natural processes, along with their claims to divine liaisons, allowed them to effectively organize the land's agricultural potential.

As servants of the gods, the priests ate particularly well, although they were prohibited from consuming certain foods. They were partial to goose, which was beloved by both the clergy and the common people. Priests avoided eating pigs, in accordance with the widespread Middle Eastern taboo. They shunned fish as well, perhaps because it was a staple of poorer people, a wild food that had been eaten long before the beginnings of their impressive civilization. Although river fish was spurned by the priests, some wealthy citizens kept artificial ponds to raise their own stocks. Affluent Egyptians enjoyed a stunning variety of foods. Archaeologists excavating tombs have unearthed casks of wine bearing labels stamped with the date and location of their production. Like today, certain vintages were especially prized.

Perhaps the highest expression of the Egyptians' culinary ingenuity was their sophistication in baking bread. The Egyptians were the first to elevate bread baking to an art, building ovens where the loaves could cook in a sealed chamber away from the fire. Bread was a food for both wealthy and common people with countless shapes and flavors available to those who could afford them.

The process of making bread begins when yeast in the air joins together with sugars that help it grow, or ferment. A similar process occurs when brewing beer; in fact, brewers and bakers have historically worked in close proximity, using the same grains and yeasts. It is possible that brewers discovered the process of using yeast to make dough rise. The Egyptians saw the process as magical, a mysterious multiplication of resources.

One wall of the tomb of King Ramses has an elaborate drawing of the king's bakery. Workers knead the dough with their feet; then others shape loaves in a variety of styles: animals, pyramids, spirals, and spheres. The breads are uniform in size, and the production looks efficient and tightly coordinated. The stylistic precision which marks ancient Egyptian art characterized their baking techniques as well. Bakers flavored loaves with dates, honey, sesame, and spices; in fact, we know of fifty different varieties of ancient Egyptian bread.

The wealthy typically enjoyed a more varied and complex diet than the poor, but there were plenty of options available for everyone. The river teemed with fish. Aside from the priests, the rest of the population happily took advantage of this native abundance, enjoying everything from mullet to crocodiles. They preserved fish as protection against the hot climate, pickling it and pressing it into cakes.

Legumes were an important source of protein, although translators disagree about the exact identity of the variety that Greeks later referred to as the "Egyptian bean." Surely they consumed fava beans, which are a staple of the Egyptian diet even today. Chickpeas and lentils were widely cultivated throughout the region. Plenty of vegetables were available, especially onions and leeks, which added flavor to fish and bean dishes.

During hard times, the country's infrastructure took care of the needy. The Old Testament tale tells of Joseph advising the Pharaoh to stock up on grain in anticipation of seven years of drought. Joseph was not suggesting a new policy, but rather predicting that an existing institution would be particularly important during the upcoming period and advocating preemptive action.

According to the biblical account of the Egyptian famine, government officials did not distribute their stockpiled grain as charity, but rather sold it to the starving people, taking what little they had in exchange. First the hungry people traded their cattle; then they turned over their silver. When they had nothing else to offer, the Pharaoh took their land, forcing them to move to the cities. Joseph interceded on their behalf and worked out an arrangement where the land still ultimately belonged to the Pharaoh, but the people were allowed to farm it. The farmers kept eighty percent of the yield, paying the remaining twenty percent to the throne.

It is curious to find this account in the Hebrew Bible, the religious canon of a neighboring land. Perhaps it appears there because the mediator between Pharaoh and his people belonged to the Hebrew tribe. Whether or not it is historically accurate, it is noteworthy that the negotiated arrangement allowed the people to keep a far greater share of their harvest than the one-third that Babylonian peasants retained under the code of Hammurabi.

THE CULTURE OF the ancient Israelites began to emerge around 1200 BC, a time of great social and cultural disturbance throughout the region. We don't know the precise reasons for these upheavals, which may have been related to climatic changes which made the region more arid and less fertile. The Egyptian and Hittite empires, which had dominated the area militarily, grew considerably less powerful. Out of this confused political environment, the tribes in ancient Israel began to unite and forge a cultural identity.

Biblical stories trace the origin of the ancient Israelites to both Mesopotamia and Egypt. According to Old Testament stories, Abraham migrated to Canaan from the land of Ur at a prompt from his god, and his descendants lived in Egypt for a spell following a severe drought. Abraham's journey from his birthplace led to the birth of the tribe, and the sojourn in Egypt was in effect a rebirth. The exodus from that land led to the gift of the law on Mount Sinai and the Israelites' ascendancy as the dominant ethnic group in their homeland of Canaan.

Archaeologists have found no evidence linking the ancient Israelites to either of these regional powers. Rather, the ancient Israelite kingdom was the product of a confederation of Canaanite tribes who probably joined together for practical reasons, perhaps in response to the environmental crisis. Over time this utilitarian arrangement evolved into a sophisticated spiritual and legal system whose legacy endures to this day.

The stories which make up the Hebrew Bible–and the Old Testament of the Christian text–were assembled from older tales. This editorial process probably started during the reign of King Solomon who, along with his father, King David, effectively united the diverse tribes occupying the land. David's contribution was mostly military, but Solomon made his mark culturally as well. He built the first temple in Jerusalem and commissioned scribes to collect the mythologies of the peoples he governed and weave a coherent tale. Future scholars compiled and added to the work, which took on a new significance when the kingdom of Israel was conquered by the Babylonian superpower, and her people were taken to live in exile there. Their sacred text then became a way to preserve their cultural heritage while living in a foreign land.

Biblical dietary laws helped to preserve the unique tradition which the ancient Israelites so vigorously defended. The prohibition against eating meat and dairy products together came from the biblical injunction against seething a lamb in its mother's milk, a practice common among neighboring tribes. Over time this proscription evolved into the modern practice of not eating meat and dairy products within several hours of each other, and even keeping different sets of dishes to separate them. At their most extreme, these rules serve to maintain an insulated community, one which hesitates to even eat with outsiders.

The anthropologist Mary Douglas, in her seminal work *Purity and Danger*, describes how the rituals and conventions of many cultures involve avoiding things which do not fit neatly into categories. Most of the animals which Old Testament dietary laws designate as unclean defy traditional notions of zoological propriety. Insects fly, but they also have legs; therefore, they are unclean. Ruminants, like cows, should have split hooves. Camels do not; therefore, they are not suitable for human consumption.

As Douglas has shown, there seems to be an innate human tendency to embrace situations that we can neatly understand and reject circumstances that are murkier. For a nation struggling to maintain its identity in exile, these prohibitions took on another level of symbolic meaning, not only representing a way to avoid the danger inherent in the unknown but also offering protection against cultural annihilation by maintaining a separate identity.

The dietary laws had a spiritual function as well. Like the cave paintings of the Paleolithic hunters and the sacred bulls and seeds of Catalhoyok, these laws infused the everyday act of eating with spiritual significance. Old Testament dietary laws place a strong emphasis on purity, which is the condition of being clean, untouched, or unadulterated. Spiritual pursuit of an ideal of purity grows out of an awareness that we are capable of making ourselves better than we are. Apart from separating the Hebrew tribe from neighboring cultures, their quest for purity elevated observant individuals above the pettiness and messiness of the world.

For the ancient people living by the law of the Old Testament, this ideal of self-improvement was more than just a way to commune with god; it was also an ethic governing interpersonal relationships. Ancient Hebrew society was more egalitarian than most others in the region. Excavated houses do not differ dramatically in size, suggesting the absence of the dramatic social and economic inequities found in neighboring cultures. The biblical laws governing land ownership offer a clue to how the Israelites prevented such gross disparities in wealth.

As we have seen, much of the consolidation of wealth in ancient Sumer occurred because families falling on hard times lost their land. During the drought described in the Bible many Egyptians, similarly, lost their property, although they were able to keep a greater share of their harvest. But the Hebrew tradition forbade the consolidation of land holdings. According to the custom of the Jubilee Year, every fiftieth year plots that had changed hands were returned to their original owners. This mandate prevented the emergence of a class of exploited, landless wage laborers and ensured a reasonably just society.

The Bible also contains laws and decrees concerning the practice of charity. Each individual was responsible for making sure that others were fed. The book of Genesis tells the tale of the patriarch Abraham encountering three strangers traveling in the desert. He welcomes them, washes their feet, and brings them food and water. They turn out to be messengers of God, bearing the message that his aging, barren wife will give birth to a son. The moral of the story is clear: take care of strangers because any one of them could be an angel carrying an important communication.

The Bible's day-to-day laws mandating charity are useful, practical measures. Any one of us could fall into hard times, and it's good to have a social safety net. One provision in the book of Leviticus requires that farmers leave the corners of their fields uncut so those in need could glean. The biblical character of Ruth, in the book that bears her name, gathers this very wheat. She goes on to bear a son who is an ancestor of the great King David, who in turn will be an ancestor of the Messiah. This mythological legacy suggests that there is nothing shameful about accepting charity. Even those who are forced to rely on the kindness of others can go on to foster royalty.

The conviction that everyone should have enough to eat is a matter of basic human decency. Without it, any kind of ritual sacrifice or religious observance is hollow and meaningless. There is a Jewish legend about the rabbi Hillel, who lived during Roman times, long after the laws of the Bible had been codified. A Roman soldier, taunting him, dared him to recite the entire Bible while standing on one leg. Hillel assumed the position and said, "Do unto others as you would have them do unto you. The rest is commentary."

Hillel's insight was especially relevant during Roman times, when the inequities that accompanied efficient, centralized food production fueled the world's first transcontinental empire. The political and military achievements of the Roman Empire brought her citizens a dazzling array of foods from an impressive geographical range. For the rich, these items offered pleasure and prestige. For priests and thinkers, they provided material for reflection and celebration. Meanwhile, the poor toiled to feed powerful armies and provision a sophisticated system of trade, while enjoying few benefits themselves.

Classical Cuisine

A WELL-KNOWN GREEK MYTH tells of the god of the underworld abducting a maiden named Persephone as she played in a narcissus field. Her mother, Demeter—the goddess of grain—went into mourning, and while she grieved, no crops grew. After persistent cajoling and persuasion, Demeter convinced Zeus to intervene on her behalf. Together they secured Persephone's release but, before letting her go, the king of Hades forced her to eat six pomegranate seeds. This obligated her to stay in the underworld.

Demeter and the king of Hades struck a deal. Persephone would live above ground for two-thirds of the year and in the underworld for the other third. This myth explains the seasons and the agricultural cycle: during winter, the period that Persephone spends underground, Demeter grieves, and the earth bears no produce. But when Persephone returns to her mother, the soil grows fertile again.

During her daughter's original sojourn in the underworld, Demeter had taken on the persona of a wandering old woman.

Her royalty shone through her rags, and she was hired to care for the king's son, an infant named Demophon. The child thrived under her care. In order to make him immortal, Demeter held his feet in the fire at night. But the child's biological mother caught her in the act and made her stop, so the boy remained mortal. Upon being discovered, Demeter set the child on the ground and revealed her true identity. The people built a temple in her honor.

After Persephone was returned to Demeter for most of the year, the grain goddess regretted the hardship that she had helped cause by making the earth infertile. In reparation, she gave the gift of agriculture to Triptolemos, a relative of her foster child Demophon. Riding in a chariot, he spread the new technology throughout the land. In one version of the story, the people began to walk upright when they received this knowledge instead of ambling on all fours as they'd previously done. Agriculture was at the heart of what it meant to be human; it separated people from animals, enabling them to stand tall.

The Eleusinian races, a Greek ritual marking the beginning of the agricultural year, celebrated the story of Demeter, Demophon, and Triptolemos. To commemorate the change from four-legged to two-legged walking, the people held races every year at Demeter's shrine. At the start of the festival, participants drank a crude barley brew from a sacred, primeval field which was considered the mythological home of the earliest cultivated grain. Later they ate cakes of refined, ground barley. The two different forms of barley symbolized the change in humans when they evolved from gatherers of wild plants to cultivators of domesticated crops.

Young men were the main participants in these rituals, which also served as rites of passage commemorating their transition to adulthood. In ancient Greece, young men tended herds until they were deemed ready for agriculture. Participation in these Eleusinian races marked a turning point for them as they left their youthful chores behind and assumed adult responsibilities. Similarly, the mythical events they reenacted symbolized a maturation of the community and even the human race as farming ushered in a new developmental phase with complex architecture and centralized government.

Greek myths about food tell two stories. They explain the current state of humans, food, and agriculture as a fall from an easier and simpler time, when food could be plucked from trees and no work was required. Other tales portray the advancements made possible when gods brought the people new foods and technologies. The story of Demeter and Persephone combines these two elements: food grew abundantly all year until the king of Hades' actions caused an infertile season, but then Demeter brought the people the gift of agriculture, which enabled them to provide for themselves.

Both types of story are consistent with the human past. As we have seen, there was once a period when food could be acquired without the hard labor of farming, but once agriculture began in earnest, it spawned the first civilizations. Like Demeter's story, the myth of Prometheus stealing fire tells of both a loss and a gift. Humans ate at the rich table of the gods until Zeus grew jealous of them. By virtue of his own error, humans had received the better part of an ox which the Titan Prometheus had divided for them all to enjoy. Zeus confiscated man's fire, but Prometheus, concerned for man's welfare, stole it back from Zeus and brought it to man in a fennel stalk.

Zeus retaliated by creating the first woman, Pandora, and by forcing humans to cultivate their own food by farming. In spite of its misogynist message, the tale tacitly acknowledges that, without woman, the human race could not reproduce just as, without agriculture, we would have no control over our food supply. Man may resent and lament these developments, but they civilize him.

The earliest phase of cohesive Greek history began around 1500 BC. This period is known as the Mycenaean Age, after an ethnic group that probably came to the mainland from Minoan Crete. They excelled primarily as a war machine, building elaborate fortifications and riding in chariots. They also controlled the seas, traveling to distant lands to fight and trade. They were originally pastoralists, or herders. The Mycenaean warlords themselves took little interest in agriculture, preferring more glamorous pursuits like raiding foreign territories and herding cattle. They did grow a limited range of crops on the Greek mainland, using flat parcels that were easy to till and enlisting the native population as laborers.

Over time Mycenaean culture and agriculture stagnated. The people tilling the ground had no incentive to improve their methods. The plots they worked weren't their own, and the warrior land owners were too distracted by military adventures to think about nurturing the soil. Overseas trading deteriorated as well, as the Mycenaeans grew accustomed to taking goods by force rather than trading for them fairly. Like the Greek tenant farmers, foreign producers were not motivated to create quality goods because they had no personal investment in their work. As it became too much effort for the Mycenaean military machine to assert its hegemony over unwilling subjects, their empire unraveled.

The country entered a period known as the Dark Age, which lasted from about 1100 BC to about 700BC. We know relatively little about this time, except that the population was sparse and there wasn't much political unity. The Greeks of this period left few of the artifacts that archaeologists traditionally look for, such as pottery and written documents. But we can glean some insights about how people lived from the culture that was firmly in place by the beginning of the Archaic Age, the period that followed.

The works of Homer and Hesiod belong to the Archaic Age. The writings of both poets describe men laboring to establish farms. As we have seen, the Mycenaeans had claimed most of the flat, fertile areas that were easy to till. Their descendants held on to these plots. The rest of the countryside was hilly and rocky, terrain that could be worked, but not easily and certainly not on an industrial scale. Just as the challenging topography of ancient Mesopotamia led to the sophisticated political organization of that land, the stony hills of ancient Greece gave birth to a fledgling democracy.

This was a landscape that could only be made productive through the initiative of determined, hardworking individuals committed to building something of value that they could pass on to their descendants. In addition to wheat and barley, the land's primary crops were olives and grapes, which could be processed into olive oil and wine. Both olive trees and grapevines thrive on the type of marginal terrain that was available to these early Greek farmers, but they need considerable attention and take years to get established. They are uniquely suited to patient, independent, hardworking farmers rather than centralized establishments seeking short term gain.

Cultivation of grape and olive trees is much more complicated than growing grains and legumes, and it takes time to learn to do it right. Unlike wheat, which follows an annual cycle, grapevines live for decades, and olive trees survive for hundreds of years. Innovations that prolong the life of these plants may not be obvious to the present generation of farmers, and it can take years to recover from mistakes. If a freak storm or a human error kills a plant or a grove, it cannot be quickly or easily replaced.

The cultivation of wine grapes, in particular, requires detailed knowledge of how different plants behave on various types of ground. Wind is factor, as is drainage. The farmer also needs to know the best time to harvest, a calculation that involves predicting fickle weather patterns. Picking early ensures that the fruit will be off the vine before a big rain comes and destroys it, but later picking can create a superior product. In fact, wine made from grapes grown on marginal soils and in harsh conditions has considerably more character than vintages made from grapes that have experienced no stress.

Both olives and grapes lend themselves to processing that enhances their value. Olives are inedible unless they are salted and preserved, and they can be pressed into the rich oil which was one of the most important commercial products in the ancient world. Grapes are far more valuable as wine than as table fruit. In addition to adding value, these processes extend the shelf life of perishable products. Farmers could process and store their wares without the added pressure of needing to bring them to town before they deteriorated. They could also weather the seemingly arbitrary fluctuations in market prices, which still plague farmers today.

As they built these modest, valuable legacies, Greek farmers also came together and created legal and political institutions reflecting their unique strengths. The Greek *polis*, or city-state, was a political institution where independent farmers wielded the greatest share of political power, using their collective voice to pass laws upholding their values and interests. The very idea of democracy, which began to emerge at this time, was a radical change from the rigid, hierarchical systems of government which prevailed elsewhere. The idea that a broad base of citizens could make political decisions could only have come out of an economic system where a sizable share of the population controlled the terms of their own livelihood, making autonomous decisions about what to grow, where to grow it, when to harvest it, and how to handle it in order to produce the most valuable, high quality food.

In some Greek city-states only persons who owned land were given a voice and a vote. This system was a vast improvement over traditional regimes where decisions were made solely by kings and priests, but it still discriminated against city dwellers and wage laborers who did not own land. Other city-states allowed all free males to vote, disenfranchising slaves and women. These exclusions are not surprising: two thousand years later, we still struggle with inequities surrounding who is entitled to a political voice.

Although Greek farmers achieved autonomy and political status unrivalled by their peers elsewhere in the ancient world, they struggled to maintain their position and could be chauvinistic themselves. They disdained not only those who had less than them but also those who had more, the aristocrats who had never learned the value of hard work. The politics and culture of the Greek city-states betrayed an ongoing tension between those citizens who were able to consolidate wealth and power through personal success or family legacy and those farmers who earned a modest, respectable living on their own terms. There was a similar struggle between independent agriculturalists and landless workers.

Some of the most enduring Greek political and intellectual achievements grew out of these class conflicts. In 594 BC, the people of Athens responded to a growing crisis between wealthy aristocrats and small-scale farmers by appointing a thinker named Solon as a special magistrate. He was well traveled and had studied a wide range of political systems. His reforms stressed the importance of balance, especially between the different factions of society.

Solon passed legislation cancelling the debts of farmers struggling to keep their land and allowed any man who could produce two hundred bushels of wine, grain, or oil to hold public office. Private citizens were allowed to prosecute city officials who had treated them unfairly. Solon inscribed these new laws on a pair of tablets and set them out for public display. These changes caused a considerable backlash among the privileged citizens of Athens and were not entirely successful in the short term. They did, however, set the stage for important developments in Greek thought, which stressed moderation and balance. The Greeks applied this ideal to everything from state institutions—which included people from a range of social classes—to their ethic of eating, which stressed the importance of consuming neither too much nor too little.

Against this backdrop of small-scale landowners struggling to retain their autonomy and their voice, the Greek city-states grew embroiled in a series of wars starting in 499 BC. They successfully fought off several invasions from the Persian Empire, which ruled much of the region. The Greeks prevailed against the stronger military power in part because they fought on their own soil, on terrain that was perfect for the military tactics, which they had perfected during the preceding centuries.

During the so called Archaic Age, the golden age of Greek agriculture, groups of farmers had periodically gone to war against neighboring communities, skirmishing over land. They fought by forming tightly knit groups of infantry, whose units locked together their large and heavy shields as they charged against similarly configured opposing forces. These conflicts tended to be brief, usually lasting no longer than a day. The equipment was inexpensive, the soldiers were citizen farmers rather than paid infantry, and the loss of life was minimal compared to other types of warfare. This egalitarian style of warfare was instrumental in shaping the self-image of these independent farmers and creating the mindset that enabled them to build the earliest democratic institutions.

This style of fighting, known as hoplite warfare, always took place by mutual agreement on relatively flat ground, where columns of forces could assemble in an orderly fashion. Such consensus was possible with battles that took place between armies that were culturally similar, sharing a region and an agricultural ethic. This was not the case when the Persian army invaded Greece, but fortunately for these hoplite soldiers, the two sides happened to face off on relatively flat ground, where the Persian invaders didn't stand a chance against the concentrated, well-protected forces charging in their direction.

Despite the fact that the Greeks successfully fought off the Persians, Greek society was never the same after these wars. They'd seen the potential of a diversified army, powerful at sea as well as on land, and they glimpsed an imperial foreign culture whose military might had united people, knowledge, and products from far-flung places. As a result of having been invaded themselves, the Greeks acquired a taste for overseas expansion.

During the years following the Persian Wars, foreign trade became increasingly important to the Greeks. Athens controlled territory on both sides of the Aegean Sea. Successful merchants exported grain, wheat, and olive oil, and they imported spices from as far away as India. The fruit-growing countries to the east were adept at drying their products to survive long sea voyages, and the Greeks traded for these items as well.

Overseas trading proved more lucrative than small-scale farming. Many of the families who had established themselves comfortably on modest parcels of land during the preceding centuries shifted gears and began earning their fortunes through commerce. Although the philosophers and poets of the period continued to praise the hardworking farmer, the culture as a whole was changing, with successful entrepreneurs accumulating fortunes using their wits and their capital rather than their hands.

The size of individual estates began to grow. During the sixth century BC, laws in Athens limited the size of each family's land holdings. The countryside was divided into farms of roughly ten acres. During the centuries that followed, enterprising farmers acquired consolidated tracts of property spanning as many as a hundred, and later a thousand, acres. These were no longer farms that could be worked by an individual along with his family and a slave or two. They were manned by the growing class of landless workers, as well as an increasing number of slaves.

As the gap between the rich and the poor widened, their diets diverged as well. The wealthy feasted on fine, imported foods while the poor subsisted on grain. The ancient Greek thinkers who wrote about the best way to eat were largely reacting to the excess they witnessed among their affluent compatriots. Pythagoras, best known for his geometrical theorems, was actually a spiritual teacher with a considerable following. He preached about the merits of an ascetic life, recommending a diet of barley bread and water.

Pythagoras believed in the immortality of the soul, and its successive reincarnation in a series of bodies. For him, the life of the soul was considerably more important than the physical body's tenure on earth. His ideas were influenced—directly or indirectly—by those of the Persian prophet Zoroaster, whose vision of the great battle between good and evil evolved over time into the Western idea of dualism, or the split between the body and the soul. For Pythagoras, the physical body should receive only the bare minimum necessary to keep it alive.

A century and a half after Pythagoras, another thinker named Epicurus recommended the same diet of barley bread and water but for very different reasons. Epicurus believed that the aim of life was to maximize pleasure and minimize pain; in fact, his name has become synonymous with excess and indulgence. But he actually taught that the greatest amount of pleasure and the smallest amount of pain could be achieved by eating a simple diet, one that would result in optimal health. Pythagoras recommended a plain diet as a way to nourish the soul apart from the physical world while Epicurus saw simple eating as a strategy benefitting the body.

Both Plato and Aristotle, the giants of ancient Greek thought, recommended a diet neither too decadent nor too austere. Like Pythagoras and Epicurus, they advocated similar styles of eating for different reasons. Plato believed that moderate eating habits were the most effective way to imitate or participate in the ideal world of forms, which was a more perfect and real version of the world at hand. Aristotle believed that the middle way, or the "Golden Mean," was the best way to strive for the worldly perfection. He also applied the idea of the Golden Mean when discussing the ideal size of a farm's acreage which, as he had seen, was an idea with widespread political implications.

While the philosophers wrote of the broad ideas behind their dietary recommendations, another group of Greek thinkers were more specific in detailing the practical merits and dangers of a wide variety of foods. The two most important Greek culinary thinkers, Athenaeus and Galen, wrote during the second and third centuries AD, when Greece had already become a Roman colony. Athenaeus wrote an encyclopedic work called *The Deipnonsophists.* Its title roughly translates as "The Food Philosophers." The part of his work which has been preserved spans thousands of pages and is poorly organized and difficult to read. It is structured as a Platonic dialogue set at an elaborate meal which is a prop to impart information about everything the Greeks knew about food, from different varieties of fish and produce to the pros and cons of various cooking appliances and the quality of preparations created using a range of cooking techniques. The work also describes the intricate choreography of a Greek feast, which included musical and theatrical entertainment, elaborate décor, and, of course, philosophical discussion.

The other important source of information about Greek food was a physician named Galen. He was a great traveler, visiting locations all over the ancient world and cataloguing their specialties. Unlike his predecessor Hippocrates who wrote about food largely as medicine, Galen was interested in the foods themselves and the pleasure that could be derived from eating them. His surviving works are extensive; in fact, they provided the basis for Western medical knowledge up until the Renaissance. Arab doctors and scholars later studied and embellished his work, translating it from Greek to Arabic, where it became the foundation for their own canon. The Jewish physician and scholar Maimonides also expounded on his writings, and Christian monks holed up in monasteries throughout medieval Europe translated his books into their native tongues.

Galen catalogued earlier Greek medical knowledge about food, incorporating the insights of Hippocrates as well as Diokles of Karystos, Mnesitheos of Athens, and Praxagoras of Kos. He favored Greek physicians from the third century BC, five hundred years before his time. But the main body of his work is devoted to personal observations, which include favorable and unfavorable reactions to foods he encountered on his travels.

He clearly loved eating and wrote about where to find the sweetest honey and the best bread. Unlike Athenaeus, who devoted his attention to sumptuous foods eaten by people with means, Galen carefully observed and evaluated the diets of poor and rural folk. He noted the negative health effects of foods that peasants were forced to eat when they could not afford their regular fare. He described a well-born child feeding from a wet nurse of a lower class and developing ulcers all over his body. Galen attributed the child's skin condition to the wild herbs that the woman—and others of her class—were likely to eat, observing that they, too, were prone to skin conditions.

He also related an incident where he was travelling in the countryside and came upon a group of peasants preparing a wheaten porridge. They shared it with him, admitting that they were only preparing it this way—rather than grinding the wheat into flour to make bread—because times were hard. Galen experienced flatulence and an upset stomach from the porridge, confirming his notion that the poor ate substandard and unhealthy food because they could not afford anything better.

Despite his negative opinions about the subsistence fare of peasants, Galen did believe that it was healthier to live and eat in the countryside than in the city. He reserved his most scathing criticisms for Rome, which during his day ruled the Mediterranean world and much of Europe, the Middle East, and North Africa. Rome was the most metropolitan city the ancient world had ever seen, bringing together foods and customs from her many colonies. The streets were crowded, and the wealthy lived a life of excess and decadence, especially in their eating habits.

The Romans came to power by virtue of their military expertise, which required extraordinary discipline. Their organizational prowess led them to build impressive and enduring public works as well as a legal system whose legacy still endures. Yet, once they began to reap the fruits of their labors, the products, riches, and slave labor from all over the empire, they also pursued pleasure to the fullest. The eating habits of the upper classes were especially hedonistic. The voluminous writings they left show them continually negotiating the tension between pleasure and duty, just as the Greeks before them had based their art, food, and philosophy on the idea of balance.

Unlike the Greeks, the Romans were deeply practical. They did not strive for order because it represented some worldly or otherworldly ideal but because it produced the best results in both everyday and unusual situations. Tales of early Roman leaders tell of a series of successful military men grabbing too much power. When their subjects objected, threatening the leaders' hegemony, the rulers eventually relented and shared authority. Some of the figures starring in these dramas were no doubt partly mythical; nonetheless, the fact that the Roman people created legends around the figure of a ruler forced to share power shows us that this was an issue close to their hearts.

Rome became an international power after winning the long and grueling Punic Wars against Carthage during the third century BC. Like Greece, Rome built a fleet and became a naval power to gain the upper hand in a regional conflict and was changed forever by the new horizons opened by overseas expansion. The victory in the Punic Wars brought a quarter of a million slaves into the Roman republic, dramatically changing the economic landscape. The availability of cheap labor favored large-scale, wealthy landowners who could now farm tremendous acreages. This situation harmed smaller-scale farmers, who relied on the work of family members and could no longer compete. In a drama which began long before the rise of Rome and continues even until this day, many independent agriculturalists lost their land.

Many of these displaced farmers moved to the cities and towns, where they worked for wages or became craftspeople or merchants. The government instituted a policy of distributing grain, and later bread, which helped to quell some of the social unrest which naturally brewed as Roman society grew increasingly stratified. The poet Juvenal called this practice "bread and circus," linking the food subsidies with the free, gory entertainment provided by government-sponsored gladiator shows.

Much of the grain used to feed the Roman republic grew in the fertile Nile valley, which came under Roman control after the Punic Wars with Carthage. As Rome conquered most of the Mediterranean world during the last two centuries BC, she often entered into mutually beneficial arrangements with her territories, treating them as partners rather than as colonies, whose resources could be extracted at will. But there were exceptions, such as the city of Carthage, which the Roman army razed to the ground.

The land of Egypt, being the breadbasket of the ancient world, also offered too important a resource to be given much autonomy. Rome ruled Egypt directly, rather than allowing the Egyptian people to set up their own governor. Roman emperors spent a disproportionate amount of time making sure that their rule over Egypt was secure. In the later years of the empire when the Vandals took control over Egypt, Rome was doomed.

During Roman times, Tunisia and Algeria, as well, were covered with wheat fields. After the conquest of Carthage, Roman soldiers were encouraged to settle and farm there. Their government assisted them by setting up cisterns and irrigation systems capable of watering huge swaths of farmland. The area grew successful and productive until its residents experienced the same difficulties plaguing small-scale farmers back in Rome. The most successful landowners gradually swallowed up the property of their smaller neighbors, amassing larger and more productive plots. By 50 BC, almost half of North Africa belonged to a handful of rich Roman families and only a few dirt farmers remained.

Meanwhile, back on the Italian peninsula, the plight of the independent farmers spawned civil unrest. A pair of brothers, Tiberius and Gaius Sempronius Gracchus, who each held the high government post of tribunal, tried to instigate land reform so that poorer farmers, especially former soldiers, had a fighting chance of making a living from their land. Both brothers were assassinated, leaving in their wake a restless and discontented populace which increased the need for a more powerful government to control them.

The first century BC was a tumultuous time. In the end, the Roman state emerged even more powerful than before, ruled by an emperor with the support of the senate. The first few centuries of the new empire were prosperous with some fine leaders, such as Augustus Caesar and Marcus Aurelius, and some decadent ones, such as Nero and Caligula. Rome now ruled colonies from what is now England to parts of modern-day Germany, as well as the Baltic region and North Africa. Trade flourished, in part because the Romans were skilled road builders who understood that they needed a solid infrastructure in order for goods to move freely across their expansive domain.

As we have seen, the average Roman citizen had ready access to government-subsidized bread. The state also ensured that everyone had an ample supply of salt, which, like bread, was viewed as a necessity. The poor ate the smaller, cheaper fish that swam the Mediterranean, preserved by salting to counter the daunting logistics of marketing them fresh. Sardines and mackerel were also salted and fermented to create a fish sauce called garum, or silphium, used in most Roman recipes; they even ate it with fruit. There were better and worse grades of fish sauce, whose production was both a cottage industry and a full-blown entrepreneurial endeavor, with major producers shipping it all over the empire.

The Romans were passionate devotees of the written word, so it is fitting that they penned the oldest surviving cookbook. *De re coquinaria*, or "On Cooking," is attributed to a famous, wealthy gourmet named Apicius, who taught haute cuisine during the first half century AD, under the reigns of Tiberius and Augustus. According to the writings of Seneca, Apicius committed suicide when he learned that he had squandered his fortune and could no longer eat in the manner to which he was accustomed.

The actual manuscript that has come down to us was copied during medieval times, and most scholars concur that it is not strictly the work of Apicius, but rather a collection of recipes by his contemporaries. Whoever the exact author, the work gives us a vivid taste of the cuisine of the time, showing us just how complex and sophisticated it had become. It contains four hundred and seventy recipes, with sections on fish, fowl, and gardening, among other topics. There is an entire chapter on fish sauces, another targeted towards farmers with instructions for preserving different foods, and one focusing on the medical use of food.

The recipes tend to have far longer lists of ingredients than contemporary cookbooks. This has led to a widespread impression that Roman cuisine was unnecessarily ostentatious, a vehicle for the wealthy to show off their good fortune. But one could come to a similar conclusion about our own cuisine if they were basing their judgment solely on the works of some of our best-known celebrity chefs.

The most famous account of conspicuous consumption in Roman cuisine comes from a satirical account of a banquet, Petronius' *Satyricon*. The host is a former slave named Trimalchio who has grown quite rich and is portrayed as an embodiment of poor taste. He serves a lavish meal, which includes such extravagances as a tray with the signs of the zodiac with a different organ meat placed on each constellation. This dish is removed and underneath it sits a pot with fowl, sows' udders, and a hare with wings dressed to look like Pegasus. Trimalchio serves dormice dipped in honey, a whole roast boar decorated with baby boars made of pastry, and a wild sow stuffed with living thrushes.

Guests wash their hands in ice water—a rare luxury—and later in wine. Trimalchio's poor taste is evident. He seats himself in the spot that is supposed to be reserved for the most honored guest and brags about the cost of the meal. He serves hundred-year-old wine, an exaggeration that poked fun at the upper-class Roman enthusiasm for aged vintages.

While Petronius' description of Trimalchio's banquet is fictional and satirical, it could not have worked effectively as satire unless some of the behaviors it mocked were actually familiar to the audience. Some Roman banquets were, in fact, scenes of incredible excess and bizarre theater. One historical account describes a meal staged by the Emperor Domitian with the theme of Hell. All of the food served was black, and the guests sat next to tombstones engraved with their names.

It's easy to speculate that the Roman Empire declined and fell because of these kinds of excesses. In fact, some Roman emperors did jeopardize the financial health of the land with their extravagances. But Rome's deterioration didn't have a single cause. Her population declined in part because it included so many slaves, and people in captivity do not reproduce at the same rate as freemen. Epidemics also took their toll. The sheer size of the empire's territory may have helped precipitate its decline: it proved virtually impossible to maintain order indefinitely over such a vast area.

As northern tribes mounted repeated assaults on the capital city of Rome, the Emperor Constantine moved the empire's seat of power to eastern Turkey. He founded the city of Constantinople, or modern-day Istanbul, which maintained the legacy of Roman culture until the fourteenth century when it became part of the Islamic Empire. Like the city of Rome in her heyday, Constantinople became a center of trade, moving foods and durable goods from the East to the West. During later years, its merchants were instrumental in bringing some of the color and vibrancy of early Islamic culture to the harsh, stagnant world of medieval Europe.

Monastic Meals and Byzantine Bread

THE NORTHERN TRIBES who brought Rome to her knees during the fourth and fifth centuries were skilled fighters, but they knew little about building, governing, or growing food. During the early years of their rule, roads went to ruin, cities emptied, and a narrow, insulated economy replaced an international trading network. In this new landscape, there was little room for small-scale farmers, traders, and artisans. The powerful church held on to vast tracts of land, but the rest of the countryside fell into the hands of rich landowners and strong warlords who formed fortified, self-sufficient domains.

At first slavery was common, especially during the period immediately following the end of the empire. As time went on, feudalism evolved as a system which gave the peasants more personal autonomy. Serfs could work a piece of land and, if they were lucky, pass on its title to their descendants. They kept most of the produce they grew, and they could not be frivolously evicted. Lords offered personal protection to peasants against roving gangs of bandits and military incursions from neighboring manors. In exchange for land, equipment, and protection, serfs provided property owners with agricultural labor and a share of their harvests.

Feudalism was a system with so many different variations that some scholars argue over whether it was a system at all. It changed over time and took different forms in diverse regions with varying agricultural traditions. No doubt the personalities of individual lords, vassals, and serfs also played a part in shaping unique arrangements with kinder land owners extending more favorable terms to their tenants.

Studies by forensic archaeologists show that medieval peasants ate reasonably well, at least better than people of the same class during earlier and later eras. They drew their foods from a wide range of sources, from the planted fields that were the pride of the Romans to the lush woods where the Germanic tribes had traditionally hunted and gathered wild plants. They grew vegetables in kitchen gardens near their cottages. The diversity of their diets was insurance against hunger: if one strategy failed, they could rely on another. The landowners also ate well. As they deeded away pieces of their estates, they ceded the responsibility for overseeing daily details of management and agriculture, leaving them with extra time to hunt and feast.

These luxuries were short-term benefits. As feudal estates proliferated, the economy and culture of Western Europe stagnated. Much of the agricultural knowledge developed by the Greeks and Romans—systems of crop rotation, care for the soil, and nuances of tending different kinds of plants—was lost or abandoned. The serfs who farmed the land lacked the technology and the incentive to nurture it and build its productivity. The only fertilizer available was manure, and there wasn't much of it. Peasants practiced crop rotation by letting fields lie fallow every second or third year, but they repeatedly planted the same crops in the same soil, exhausting its nutrients and growing produce which probably did not provide much nourishment.

Although agricultural knowledge in Europe was primitive during the early Middle Ages, farming became a way of life even in lands that had previously been pastoral. The people who ultimately transformed the food economies of the northern lands were warriors and chiefs returning from the south. Like the warlords who invaded the ailing Roman Empire, they were interested mainly in personal gain. Their experience as fighters did not prepare them for the patient work of nurturing a piece of land over time, getting to know its idiosyncrasies, and weathering adverse seasons. Agriculture in these areas was not especially productive, and the serfs who worked the land lived harsh and difficult lives.

They produced most of what they needed for themselves because trade and commerce were limited. As Roman roads and bridges deteriorated, it became difficult to get from place to place carrying goods. Travelers were plagued by bands of thieves and exorbitant tolls. Trade was also constricted by the lack of a common currency. Shaky governments did not have enough precious metal to mint coins, and their currency didn't always contain consistent amounts of gold. Without a stable, consistent medium of exchange, commerce generally took the form of barter, which limited its possibilities.

Things were different in Byzantium, the eastern remnant of the Roman Empire. The government there managed to hang on to much of its power even as the infrastructure in the west unraveled. Witnessing the rise of warlords and feudal estates throughout Europe, the Byzantine government took preemptive steps to limit the power of wealthy aristocrats, implementing policies that strengthened the middle class and enabled

them to farm independently and thrive as autonomous artisans and merchants.

Byzantine rulers used many of the same strategies that had
been successful during the heyday of Rome. They made sure
the roads were in good working order, and they minted a stable
currency using a consistent amount of gold. Their strong naval
fleet controlled maritime commerce in the Mediterranean Sea.
Even Genoan and Venetian merchants, who eventually became
the most powerful and successful traders of the late Middle
Ages, operated under the thumb of the Byzantine Empire during its bountiful years. With a thriving economy, the citizens
of Byzantium shared a rich and diverse culture, enjoying foods
from all over the known world.

Spices were their most important culinary import. Most of
these valuable aromatics were grown in India and Southeast Asia,
especially on the islands of Indonesia. Asian and Arab traders
brought cargoes of nutmeg, cloves, pepper, and cinnamon across
the Arabian Sea and up through the Persian Gulf. Other shipments traveled via Africa through the Gulf of Aden and along
the Red Sea, then by caravan to the Mediterranean, which linked
them to ports all over the Middle East and Europe.

Spices were exotic. Some, like nutmeg, only grew on a couple
of Southeast Asian islands, and sailors from Europe, the Middle
East, and Byzantium had not yet developed the seafaring knowledge and navigational tools to reach these places. The traders
who brought spices from distant points were secretive about their
sources. In Greek and Roman times, there had even been tales of
strange yellow men who would not meet their trading partners
face-to-face, and tremendous birds who delivered cinnamon bark
from nests in tall trees. The tradition of outlandish tales created a
mystique and a legacy which survived into medieval times.

It became the fashion for wealthy medieval households to consume copious quantities of spices. The monthly value of the aromatics they purchased exceeded the annual income of a typical serf. Some culinary historians have speculated that these lords and ladies used pounds of spices because their meat was rotten, and aggressive seasoning disguised foul tastes and smells. But wealthy people then, as now, had access to plenty of fresh meat, and spices really don't do much to hide inferior ingredients. Heavily spiced food was actually a form of conspicuous consumption in an era when class divisions were so sharp that the lower classes were barely considered human.

While the wealthy lords were flouting their riches, the medieval church was busy preserving the culture and learning of Roman times. The bishop of Rome—who eventually became known as the pope—maintained a hallowed post in the holy city. Rome held on to her religious hegemony long after the military and political power of the empire had crumbled. But the real strength of the medieval church lay not in the bishops of Rome or their rivals in Constantinople but rather in the monasteries established throughout the rural landscape.

Christian monasticism began developing as early as the third and fourth centuries AD. It grew out of the earlier tradition of solitary sojourns in the desert, which reached back at least as far as Jesus, John the Baptist, and the Hebrew Essenes. These ascetic hermits spent years alone, depriving themselves of basic comforts and social contacts. They ate just enough to survive and often inflicted physical suffering on themselves, chaining themselves to posts and whipping themselves bloody.

Christian sects proliferated during the heyday of the Roman Empire and after its decline. They struggled to make sense of the ostensible paradox behind the mysterious connection between

Christ's physical and divine sides, and they preached a wide range of solutions to this question. Their disdain for the body had a distinctly Christian aspect, but it did not grow up in isolation. It was actually part of the dualist tradition which was first preached by the Persian mystic Zoroaster at least a thousand years earlier. Like Zoroaster's spiritual descendants, who mostly consumed frugal, vegetarian diets, many early Christian sects practiced culinary abstemiousness as a way of separating themselves from the physical world.

During the last few centuries of the Roman Empire and the first few centuries after its fall, visionary monks began organizing solitary ascetics into communities. These worshippers lived apart from the world of sex, commerce, and war, but their lives weren't nearly as austere as the hermits of earlier days. The best-known early proponent of monasticism was Saint Benedict, whose followers travelled widely, establishing monasteries offering shelter and routine. Monks prayed alone for specified periods of time and also worked together, usually sharing meals. Their labor included studying the Bible and copying manuscripts, a task which proved instrumental in preserving libraries of earlier works which might not have otherwise survived.

They also cared for the poor and needy and took part in activities relating to their own day-to-day sustenance. They worked the land and tended livestock, crafting foods like cheese and wine from raw materials. While agriculture in the surrounding countryside mostly stagnated with struggling serfs eking a living out of overworked plots, these monks lovingly tilled their land and fully enjoyed its fruits.

Unlike the serfs, who focused mainly on subsistence, the monks developed specialties, sharing and preserving culinary knowledge for future members of their orders. Their diets were mostly—but not completely—vegetarian, in part because church authorities mandated numerous ceremonial fast days. For medieval monks, "fasting" meant avoiding animal products except fish and sometimes eggs. The number of fast days in any given year varied, especially in accordance with the current availability of meat and dairy. Many religious laypeople followed these mandates as well.

This link between shunning meat and living a life of the spirit was in part a reaction to a long-standing tradition linking meat and power. Medieval lords took their sport hunting seriously and passed laws forbidding people of lower classes from competing for game. Even the great king Charlemagne, who was a great supporter of piety and learning, was partial to spit-roasted meat. By choosing not to eat meat, at least on certain days, these monks—and observant laypeople following the same regimen— were making a statement about their lack of interest in worldly wealth and prestige.

Despite the fact that they ate little meat, the monks ate much better than the average citizen, gracefully balancing the abstention from particular foods with a robust enjoyment of those items they were allowed. At its best, their diet must have been a rich metaphor for the spiritual life they chose, which involved renouncing all kinds of worldly pleasures while offering a host of spiritual benefits in their place. At their worst, these meals could have been cynical grabs at the practical advantages made possible by the wealth and power of the church. No doubt the sincerity of the practice varied from individual to individual and from monastery to monastery.

The list of plants grown in the kitchen garden of one Carolingian monastery included sage, fennel, chervil, pennyroyal, lovage, mint, celery, horehound, rosemary, fenugreek, and catnip. The account book of another cloister mentioned trips to the market that included purchases of pepper, cinnamon, galangal, and cloves. Their food must have been complex, subtle, and lovingly prepared, a safe way for men who denied themselves sexual pleasure to derive enjoyment from the physical world.

The fact that they produced much of their food themselves, rather than sitting back and enjoying the work of servants, speaks to another aspect of their spiritual practice, much like the Eastern idea of karma yoga. Although God was most commonly associated with the spiritual world, the physical realm was undeniably his creation as well. Simple, honest work could be a way of glorifying and praising him, building knowledge through hands-on labor.

While rich feudal lords celebrated their achievements with feasts focused on binge drinking, the monks' table was a place of discipline and quiet, at least on the surface. The traditions and conventions governing what is considered proper and improper eating behavior—table manners—probably had their origins in the medieval monasteries, where monks followed strict rules about how their food was to be served and eaten. They were supposed to eat in silence, although, as one monastic visitor disapprovingly reported, they were known to converse with gestures, displaying a merriment that some sober-minded observers considered inappropriate.

Saint Benedict, the father of monasticism, was interested in creating a community which could foster a way of life that was deeply spiritual and yet not so austere as to drive away willing participants. To this end, he based the diet of his order on wine, bread, and fish. As we have seen, wheat earned a special status in ancient cultures because of gluten's special ability to interact with yeasty cultures and produce dough that rises. The medieval church layered a new level of meaning onto this age-old mystique. Bread represented the body of Christ, making it a logical choice for the monks' dietary staple. Over time the importance of wheaten bread in monastic diets—and also in the meals of religious laypersons—led to an agriculture disproportionately focused on growing wheat, despite the fact that other grains such as barley and spelt have superior yields.

In Western Europe, bread was frequently made from a mixture of wheat and rye, in ratios mostly corresponding to the relative affluence of the people who ate it. The gentry ate mostly wheat, and their grain was mostly white, having had much of the germ sifted and removed. This was a labor-intensive process that also removed nutrients. Most medieval peasants did not have mills to grind their own flour or ovens to bake it. They'd bring their grain to the miller and their flour to the baker. Each tradesman kept a portion in exchange for their services, but they often abused the privilege, keeping more than their share and adulterating the rest with sawdust or sand. The monasteries had their own mills and ovens. Monks ate plenty of good, white bread. It was a basic food, but a special one.

Wine had religious significance as well, reaching back at least as far as the Jewish tradition which spawned the Christian faith. At the Last Supper, wine symbolized the blood of Christ. Despite its sacred status, it induced a feeling a well-being and goodwill, and also intoxication when used immoderately. Since Egyptian times, vintners had been brewing especially fine wines from especially fine grapes. Its inclusion in Benedict's culinary trio tempered the sobriety of monastic life with a sanctified release, one which had deep roots in affluent, secular culture.

Wine production requires patience and is, therefore, well suited to monastic life. Monks had their eye on eternity, so the extended periods of time required for grapevines to reach maturity made sense to them. During the early days of the European monasteries, wine making was an ideal way for cloistered monks to earn a living. The protected nature of their communities allowed them to perfect the art, and they exchanged some of the finished product for necessities that they could not produce themselves. In order to protect themselves from marauding warlords, they sometimes hid their precious product underground in cellars. This led to the fortuitous discovery that vintages age better when preserved underground, and to this day, oenophiles store their collections in subterranean rooms.

Fish was the third important monastic food. It was not technically considered an animal product and was therefore permitted on fast days. Its social significance varied with the type and size: large specimens were rare and difficult to catch, fitting fare for nobility, while nearly anyone could feast on smaller fish. Since ancient Egyptian times, wealthy households had been raising stock in ponds, enjoying fresh catch even on inland estates. Fish farming was also widely practiced in medieval Europe, shaping the landscape. Monks and laypeople dug canals and ponds. Eels were especially popular. They could be kept alive out of water for several days and could therefore be shipped and stored. Lamprey and carp also lent themselves well to aquaculture.

The church prohibition against eating meat on fast days applied to all Catholics. Merchants and fishermen build a thriving trade in salted fish, especially during the late Middle Ages when improved roads and stable currency helped to revive the economy. Herring was available in staggering quantities off the Atlantic coast when it was in season. During herring season, entire villages were employed preserving the catch during the limited window of time before it spoiled.

Cod was another fish whose high oil content made it ideal for salting; in fact, some connoisseurs believe that salted cod is superior to fresh. Basque fisherman developed a lucrative cod-fishing business, building boats that could take them far out into the Atlantic, to fishing grounds whose locations they refused to divulge. It is possible that their expeditions took them as far as North America; though unlike later explorers, they had more to gain from keeping their discoveries secret than from broadcasting them to the world.

WHILE CATHOLIC MONKS were busy nurturing what was left of Roman culture, followers of the relatively new Islamic tradition were rapidly spreading their own faith, building centers of learning. The prophet Mohammed founded the Muslim faith in Arabia during the seventh century, bringing an ethic of charity and tolerance to a fierce, trading people with a long history of blood feuds. During the century after his death, his followers conquered most of the Middle East and North Africa and then spread northward into Spain and southern Italy.

Arab warriors learned hungrily from the people they came to rule. Islam had instilled in them a taste for knowledge, and there was much to glean from the Egyptians in Alexandria, the Syrians in Damascus, and the Persians in Nishapur. Unlike Christianity, Islam did not convert people by force. The people they conquered accepted the new religion willingly, embracing its ethic of tolerance and its love of learning. The religious canon of the original Muslims grew splintered very soon after the prophet's death with deep rifts emerging among his followers about who to regard as his legitimate successor. The groups ruling the far-flung territories of the early Islamic empire did not answer to a single, centralized rule, but they did enjoy a common culture, one their European neighbors feared and admired.

As European society closed in on itself, growing insulated and static, the Islamic world eagerly explored and absorbed. Philosophers, poets, astronomers, physicians, and mathematicians thrived in an environment that celebrated their achievements. The economy of the Islamic world mirrored its intellectual expansiveness. Perched on the crossroads between the East and the West, living in a land that produced little itself, the Arabs had traditionally been merchants and herders, migrating from place to place in search of trading partners and oases.

Arab traders had traditionally been middlemen between Europe and the merchants on the Indian subcontinent who wholesaled spices from their own land and also imported aromatics from further east. Using these exotic ingredients as well as seasonings grown closer to home, the people of the Islamic empire developed a cuisine that was the envy of Europe. Persian food, in particular, was highly regarded as early as Greek and Roman times, alternately admired and shunned for its lavishness.

As the Muslim world expanded to encompass present-day Iran as well as much of North Africa and parts of southern Europe, the Persian influence blended with the traditions of neighboring regions. Cooks incorporated dried fruits, almonds, sugar, sesame, spinach, leeks, saffron, ginger, and semolina pasta into their recipes, developing one of the most sophisticated culinary traditions the world has ever known. The Catholic monks who were producing most of the artisan food in the west borrowed heavily from the cuisine of the Arab world.

STARTING IN THE late eleventh century, Catholic popes and kings repeatedly raised armies and marched against the Muslim world in campaigns known as the Crusades. The ostensible goal of the early Crusades was to gain control of the holy city of Jerusalem, although control of trade routes could have been an equally important motive. The first Crusade, in 1093, successfully took the city. The conquerors were merciless, and the blood of Jews and Arabs literally flowed in the streets.

Later campaigns spanned several centuries, and they weren't nearly as triumphant or focused as the first incursion. By the time of the sixth and seventh Crusades, European kings were raising armies without the pope's sanction. They even fought against Christian Byzantium, weakening her economic and cultural hegemony and making her so vulnerable that she eventually fell to Ottoman invaders.

In addition to changing the map of Europe and the Near East, the Crusades had a profound effect on daily life throughout the region. In order to mobilize so many troops, roads needed to be rebuilt and maintained. The improved travel conditions led to a flowering of trade, creating a demand for artisan products and drawing people to the growing towns where they found the resources to build businesses.

The soldiers who had travelled to Arab lands caught a glimpse of a culture far more advanced than their own. They returned home with a taste for the foods and ways of the east. The spices that had been trickling into Europe even during its darkest times were now very much in demand, and the infrastructure to transport them was in place. Venetian and Genoan merchants rose to prominence, controlling trade in the Mediterranean as the Byzantine hold on sea routes weakened.

The period of the Crusades was also a time of agricultural innovations. Metal ploughs came into widespread use, digging deeper into the soil, and the use of a moldboard cut furrows in the ground. A new type of harness helped oxen carry heavier loads, and a three-field system of crop rotation, replacing the earlier two-field rotation, dramatically increased yields. Rocky hillsides that were difficult to farm became acreage for pasturing livestock. The manure that these cattle produced was useful as fertilizer. In turn, cover crops grown in wheat fields during alternating years could be used to feed sheep, cows, and pigs. The feudal system began to unravel as food became abundant and the population of Europe rapidly increased. The new productivity enabled the descendants of farmers to strike out on their own, moving to the towns and learning trades. The efficiency of the new farming technologies also made it profitable for property owners to manage their own lands. Whenever possible, they opted to pay workers for their time, rather than maintaining relationships that spanned lifetimes and even multiple generations.

As the nonagricultural workforce became more diversified, producers of nonfood items came to rely on the food industry for daily sustenance. Farmers traded grains, fruit, vegetables, and meat in the towns. Artisans explored ways to transform ordinary foods, making them less perishable and more interesting. They developed professional organizations to protect their market share and vest their technical skills with legitimacy. Bakers, in particular, formed guilds. Novices worked as apprentices before opening their own shops. Professional knowledge was also passed down through families.

Local governments supported the emergence of fairs and markets where local and foreign merchants could come together with consumers. They traded in handicrafts and also in food items such as grain, produce, and preserved products such as fish and dried fruits. Prepared food vendors sold meals ready to eat. These practices created a thriving economy during the first few centuries of the new millennium. The middle class enjoyed a sense of their own worth and demanded a voice. Legislation from this time recognizes the rights of individuals, who increasingly grew involved in local government.

The widespread devastation caused by the Black Plague during the fourteenth century brought an end to the broad-based prosperity of the late Middle Ages. Both workers and consumers were in short supply as some communities lost up to a third of their populations. Wages rose temporarily because labor was scarce. In England, King Edward III issued the Ordinance of Laborers in 1349, and Parliament passed the Statute of Laborers in 1351. These regulations prohibited workers from demanding more for their services than they had before the plague. Despite these decrees, the value of labor increased, but the cost of goods also rose, so the free peasants did not prosper despite their higher pay.

The gentry seems to have been hit as hard as the poorer classes by the epidemic, also losing practically a third of their populations, but they were better able to weather the financial consequences of these losses. Individual families lost property and wealth as members of their lineages died, and survivors found themselves on the wrong side of quirky inheritance laws, but the lost property was usually claimed by other wealthy families.

As the entrepreneurial middle class lost much of the property and political standing they'd gained during the late Middle Ages, a small, powerful group of extremely successful merchants and speculators emerged. Unlike the wealthy feudal lords who had secured their position largely through military means, the new gentry came to power as businesspeople. Like their precursors, they exercised an insatiable greed. They established strong ties with their governments, which increasingly acted in their interests.

Members of this successful minority offered credit to struggling landowners, seizing their property when they were unable to pay. Agricultural entrepreneurs reclaimed plots that they had previously rented to independent farmers. The collusion of business and political interests created a legal climate that sanctioned these seizures. The concentration of land in the hands of a relatively small number of people led to more efficient farming, geared towards large-scale production of a limited number of crops, often for the purpose of export rather than feeding local populations.

The newly wealthy of the late Middle Ages were eager to show off their wealth, and opulent meals were a popular medium for these displays. Members of historically powerful families in turn hosted grandiose events aimed at reasserting their privileged status. Banquets were lavish affairs, sometimes including hundreds of dishes, with dozens placed on the table simultaneously for each course. Guests were probably unable to sample everything, but these events had more to do with conspicuous consumption than with appreciation of fine food. Leftovers were donated to the poor.

These late medieval affairs generally including music and theater and were organized around themes, such as classical mythology or the culture of the Islamic world. Servers wore costumes and presented their offerings in an intricately choreographed fashion. Artists fashioned entire scenes out of spun sugar, delicacies which contained inedible colorings and binders and were probably not even meant to be eaten.

The sequence of courses and the types of dishes varied from country to country, but the tendency to closely follow established conventions when planning a menu appeared throughout the European continent. Guests were seated and served in strict compliance with their standing in society. This obsession with order corresponded with the world view that was prevalent at the time. Medieval Europeans saw the universe as strictly ordered into a hierarchy beginning with God and the angels, descending through upper- and then lower-class humans, and ending with the animal kingdom.

This ideological framework helped to keep the peasantry in their huts and the feudal lords in their castles. The order and artificiality of this structured world contrasted with the brutal and unpredictable nature of daily life for both rich and poor. Even wealthy gentry died during crippling epidemics. The decorum of medieval mealtimes, especially on festive occasions, was a comforting but illusory remnant of a safer and simpler time.

New Worlds, New Foods

URING THE LATE Middle Ages, Venetian and Genoan merchants grew phenomenally wealthy moving silks and spices into Europe from the Arab world. They built banks, patronized artists, and chose popes. Their money helped finance the construction of great churches in Rome, giving donors clout in both worldly and spiritual domains. The Catholic Church of that period also raised money for architectural projects by selling indulgences to sinners, forgiving them for misdeeds and even accepting payment in advance for future sins.

On a trip to the holy city in 1510, Martin Luther witnessed the rebuilding of St. Peter's Cathedral and was shocked by the extravagance of the project. In reaction to this type of rampant hypocrisy and excess, Luther nailed his ninety-five theses to the door of the Castle Church in Wittenberg seven years later, sparking a monumental schism in European culture and religion. His followers were fed up with the systematic corruption in the Roman Church. They also came largely from Northern Europe, where butter was the primary cooking fat. For them, the abstinence from dairy products which the Catholic Church mandated on fast days involved greater sacrifice than it did for the southern Europeans, who could cook with olive oil in their customary fashion, even on Fridays and during Lent.

Luther was committed to bringing his religion to the common people. He saw faith as a direct relationship between an individual and a deity, without a priestly intermediary. He translated the Latin Bible into German, a layman's language, and saw the importance of the newly invented printing press as a tool for spreading knowledge and empowering individuals. Printing technology lowered the cost of books, increasing the number of readers by making written material more readily available.

Printing also changed Europe's food. Like the invention of written language during Sumerian times, the printing press gave cooks new tools to preserve their art in writing for contemporaries and future generations. Despite Luther's egalitarian vision, early printed cookbooks targeted readers who could afford to hire cooks and buy specialty ingredients. The seminal French cookbook, *Le Grand Cuisinier*, which appeared in 1540, contained instructions for handling hare, swan, cormorant, capon, partridge, carp, and sturgeon, as well as instructions for planning banquets. Many recipes called for expensive, imported ingredients, especially spices.

Trade in spices mushroomed as roads that had lain in disrepair since the Dark Ages were again maintained, and knights returning from Crusades brought back a taste for eastern flavors. The merchants of Genoa and Venice thrived from this commerce, controlling shipping in the Mediterranean and maintaining networks of trading partners in the Arab world. By the end of the fifteenth century, Portugal had become a key player as well. Portugal is a small country with few natural resources. Perched on the western edge of Europe, her sailors were ideally situated to explore the oceans. Portuguese merchants grew tired of watching ships from Venice and Genoa loaded with aromatics sailing past the Portuguese capital of Lisbon bound for the wealthier cities of Brussels and Amsterdam. The Italians weren't interested in the salt and olive oil which were all the Portuguese had to trade.

Portugal's very paucity of resources drove her sailors to join risky expeditions; there were few other ways for common men to prosper. For the average seaman, the chances of dying en route to the east were high. Even on successful voyages, a tenth of a ship's crew didn't make it back alive. To counter the risk, the crown offered fringe benefits, allotting even lowly crew members one empty chest to fill. If they could afford to stuff it with expensive spices, like cinnamon and ginger, they could sell their haul back in Portugal for a sum equaling several years' wages.

During the period between 1415 and 1488, Portuguese explorers made their way down the west coast of Africa. At first they captured the Muslim city of Ceuta on the northern tip of Morocco, and then they took a series of previously uninhabited islands off Africa's northern Atlantic coast. The Azores and Madeira eventually served as important outposts for provisioning ships headed for Brazil and points east. In the short term, the Portuguese turned the islands into sugar plantations, creating a model for industrial sugar cultivation on European colonial territories.

In addition to their search for navigational routes, the Portuguese sought immediate return in gold. They did find some precious metals, but more importantly, they began trading in staples such as sugar, fish, and wheat. In West Africa, they found ample sources of malegueta pepper, or grains of paradise, a spice that was widely used during that period. They made a handsome profit importing this popular aromatic, and their success inspired them to attempt longer voyages in search of more valuable cargo. These journeys became a national priority under the sponsorship of several curious and ambitious members of the royal family. Prince Henry the Navigator sponsored multiple expeditions during the early half of the fifteenth century. King Joao II, who reigned from 1481 until 1495, also invested heavily in overseas exploration, a focus which led to important gains during his reign and helped the tiny nation to become an international power.

In addition to seeking gold, spices, and international standing, the Portuguese were also on a religious mission. Their ships carried clergymen entrusted with the task of protecting the souls of the seamen on their long journeys and also converting foreigners along the way. According to a myth circulating in Europe at the time, a king named Prester John ruled a community of Christian subjects somewhere in the Middle East. The story had been spread by a popular writer named John Mandeville, who published a travel journal in 1366. Mandeville described Prester John's amazing military victories over the heathens, and many lonely, desperate sailors searched for this protector and friend. The Portuguese did eventually find a small Christian community in East Africa, but it was hardly the powerful kingdom that Mandeville had described. Like many other stories in the travel writer's works, such as the tale of a garden of transmigrated souls, the account of Prester John's domain was probably fabricated.

The Europeans knew that the continent of Africa lay between them and India, but they did not know how large Africa was or how long it would take to sail around it. Portuguese sailors rounded Sierra Leone, a thousand miles south of Portugal, in 1480, and by 1488, Bartolomeu Diaz reached the southern tip of Africa. As they travelled farther afield, these explorers found themselves at the limits of current navigational knowledge, charting their paths in reference to unfamiliar stars. They had been relying on maps copied from those drawn by the ancient cartographer Ptolemy, but they were venturing out of the territory that he had charted, and his information was well over a thousand years old. According to Ptolemy, the Indian Ocean was a landlocked sea. Portuguese sailors also enlisted the help of Arab and Jewish astronomers, who were developing new navigational tools that enabled them to keep track of their location even out of sight of land. Some of these calculations were more successful than others, but even the failed forays added to their knowledge of how to traverse the seas.

Although Diaz was able to round the southernmost tip of Africa in 1488, Portuguese sailors did not capitalize on his discovery and sail the final stretch to India until nearly ten years later. Having learned just how far they would have to travel, they began wondering whether this was actually the most efficient route. They dispatched scouts overland to assess the trading conditions in India. They also took pause upon receiving news of another famous exploratory journey: Christopher Columbus' trip to the New World.

Columbus was a Genovese navigator who proposed sailing to the east by travelling west. Armed with the new knowledge that the world was round, and deluded by Ptolemy's assumption that its circumference was only three thousand miles rather than the actual twenty five thousand, Columbus began shopping around for a government to sponsor his exploratory journey. The Portuguese monarchy turned him down, figuring they should continue pursuing their successful journeys around Africa.

King Ferdinand and Queen Isabella of Spain agreed to support his venture, and Columbus set out on his famous voyage.

When he reached North America, the Portuguese delayed their forays eastward, hedging their bets. If Columbus had in fact reached the shores of Asia, as most people then believed, then it would be far more cost-effective to follow in his footsteps, rather than continuing with their long and arduous journeys around the southern cape of Africa.

The Portuguese crown even tried to stake a claim to Columbus' discovery. In 1479, Spain and Portugal had forged an agreement known as the Alcacovas-Toledo treaty under the pope's mediation. This agreement gave Portugal title to any land colonized "beyond Guinea." When Columbus landed on the island of Hispaniola, Portuguese emissaries argued to the pope that Spain's claim to the newly found territory violated the terms of this agreement because these previously unknown lands lay within their specified domain. In 1495, the two countries negotiated a new deal, again with the help of the pontiff. This Treaty of Tordesillas split the globe in half, drawing a line down the middle of the Atlantic Ocean. Lands to the west belonged to Spain; territories to the east were Portuguese.

With this agreement in place, the Portuguese once again set out to chart their route around Africa towards the elusive spice merchants of India. Vasco da Gama led the first successful voyage to the subcontinent, setting out in 1497 and arriving in 1498. He sailed far from the African shore, taking advantage of mid-ocean currents. His sailors stayed out of sight of land for ninety-three days, the longest open sea voyage ever completed at that time. Three years later, another Portuguese navigator, Pedro Alvarez Cabral, travelled even further westward into the Atlantic Ocean following the same currents and unwittingly landed in Brazil, which happened to lie on the Portuguese side of the line drawn by the Tordesillas treaty.

Meanwhile, da Gama rounded the southernmost tip of Africa and began making his way northward towards India. He tried trading with the people he met on the east coast of Africa, but for the most part, they were unimpressed with what he had to offer. Unlike Africa's western coast, which had not had much contact with traders until Portuguese sailors arrived, East Africa had been trafficked by merchant ships for hundreds—and even thousands—of years. The Portuguese had not anticipated such sophisticated trading partners and had not brought along anything of value to them.

When their attempts at trade proved unsuccessful, the explorers resorted to violence. They killed, tortured, and mutilated anyone who stood in their path or refused to trade on their terms. They also took advantages of age-old rivalries between factions on the Indian mainland, supporting and enriching the enemies of their enemies. Their tactics were brutal but successful, and before long they had dramatically altered the balance of power in the region.

During the fifteenth century the Portuguese became the dominant player in the European spice trade, replacing the Venetians who had controlled commerce in the Mediterranean for decades. In Venice itself, this change spurred a shift in culinary aesthetics, setting the stage for the exquisite simplicity of modern Italian cuisine. Now that their own merchants weren't profiting as heavily from the sale of spices, the citizens of Venice—and eventually all of Italy—began moving away from the heavily seasoned food of the late Middle Ages and Renaissance, and relying primarily on basic flavors and fresh, locally produced ingredients.

Spice prices fell as Portuguese expeditions returned from the east bearing their precious cargoes. Aromatics were still expensive, but more people could afford them. But the Portuguese never managed to attain a monopoly on the spice trade coming out of India, despite their best—and most brutal—efforts. They built forts and outposts and sailed yearly fleets of ships, but the market was too large and too complex for them to truly dominate.

Arab and Indian traders had been working with Southeast Asian merchants for millennia by the time the Portuguese arrived, and their ties and traditions could not be unraveled in a matter of decades. The spices reaching European markets actually represented only a small fraction of the total trade. Boatloads also went to the Middle East and India as well as to the Chinese, whose passion for exotic flavors rivaled that of the Europeans.

Eventually, Arab merchants working with Indian suppliers renewed their trading relationships with the Venetians, who picked up precious cargo in Cairo and then sailed it into Europe through the Mediterranean. Now spices were flowing into Europe through two routes. To maintain a competitive edge, the Portuguese began exploring ways to purchase aromatics directly from their source, cutting out the middleman. By 1513, they finally reached the Moluccas, the archipelago of Indonesian islands that grew all of the world's cloves.

They ran into new difficulties with Spain over these Southeast Asian islands. In 1519, Fernão de Magalhães, also known as Ferdinand Magellan, set out to once again attempt Columbus' original mission: to reach the east by travelling west. Magellan was actually Portuguese, but he couldn't convince the government of his own country to finance his voyage, so he ultimately sailed under the flag of Spain. Of the 240 men who originally sailed with him, only 18 returned to Seville three years later. They had in fact reached the east by sailing west, but the journey was farther than anyone had imagined, and it took even longer than sailing around Africa. Still, their voyage finally showed navigators the actual size of the earth's circumference.

This knowledge had a direct impact on the Treaty of Tordesillas, which had divided the globe between Spain and Portugal nearly thirty years before anyone knew the actual size of the territory they were splitting. According to geographers employed by the king of Spain, the Moluccas of present-day Indonesia lay within the Spanish domain. The Portuguese crown naturally countered the Spanish claim. In the end, the issue was decided in favor of Spain, but Spanish explorers were so busy in the western hemisphere that they sold Portugal the rights to the territory for a nominal sum.

This left the way clear for the Portuguese to trade directly with the Southeast Asian spice growers, who were just as happy to work with them as they were to do business with the Chinese and Arab traders whom they had been working with for centuries. For the most part, the Portuguese loaded their precious cargo and sailed away with it. They didn't need to wage wars and build fortresses as they'd done in India because they had few competitors bold or well provisioned enough to travel the great distance to buy their spices at their source. Cargoes returning to Portugal could fetch as much as seven hundred times what the merchants had paid for them.

This success was short lived. In 1578, Portugal came under the rule of King Phillip II of Spain, who happened to also be next in line for the Portuguese crown. His domain also included Belgium, Luxembourg, and the Netherlands. These Protestant countries were unhappy about being under the thumb of a Catholic ruler, especially a fanatically religious one. Phillip sent in troops to subdue unruly Dutch subjects, and a long and vicious war ensued. The monarch used the substantial Portuguese fleet for his military efforts, striking a blow to the nation's overseas trade, which no longer had enough vessels at its disposal.

Established traders themselves, the Dutch took advantage of this vulnerability to set sail for the Spice Islands. They were assisted by a book that had been recently published by a young Dutchman named Jan Linschoten, who had traveled to the east as a hired hand on a Portuguese vessel, and then written a best-selling work about the spice trade which included navigational charts, maps, and descriptions of the different islands, including information about where each type of spice could be found.

Unlike the Portuguese, who sailed east for religious as well as commercial reasons, the Dutch had a solid history as merchants and were clear about their mercenary objectives. While the Portuguese ships sometimes held as many clergymen as sailors, the Dutch fleets carried only the personnel they needed to man the ship, as well as cooks and doctors to take care of their basic physical needs. Their single-minded sense of purpose, along with the Portuguese naval vulnerability, enabled them to quickly become the main European spice importers.

At first there was fierce competition among individual Dutch merchants for control of trade routes. The government grew concerned that rivalry was stifling economic potential and formed the United East India Company, accepting investment capital from wealthy entrepreneurs as well as average citizens. The company created an efficient and profitable operation. The Portuguese had been content to trade with local producers in Southeast Asia, but the Dutch stopped at nothing short of razing entire islands and killing their people. To staff their plantations, they imported slaves from Africa.

Seeing the Dutch success, the English began vying for their share. The two navies fought bitterly for control of tiny islands, especially the Banda Islands where all of the world's nutmeg grew. But the English proved to be no match for the Dutch, so England turned her attention instead to new colonies in the western hemisphere.

By the middle of the seventeenth century, Europeans began losing their taste for nutmeg, cloves, cinnamon, and pepper, at least in medieval quantities. The Dutch took pains to keep prices high, even torching warehouses to avoid flooding the market, but spices had already become everyday commodities rather than trophies. The European passion for spices eventually went the way of most fads, peaking and then fading.

The death of the Dutch spice industry accelerated in 1750 when a Frenchman named Pierre Poivre smuggled clove and nutmeg seedlings from the Spice Islands and successfully propagated them on French-held islands in the Indian Ocean. Poivre's act was part of a larger trend of European nations biologically colonizing non-western lands, changing the landscape by bringing in nonnative plant and animal species.

During the eleventh century, Arab merchants and growers had begun successfully growing sugar cane in parts of the Middle East. Centuries later, the Portuguese began planting cane in their New World territory of Brazil, which had an ideal climate for the profitable crop. The work of processing sugar was hot and dangerous. The Portuguese tried enslaving the native Brazilians, but too many sickened and died. Instead they brought slaves from Africa, taking advantage of localized conflicts by forming alliances with tribes willing to sell prisoners of war into slavery. Over the next few centuries, they shipped millions of slaves to Brazil to work on their plantations, building a profitable industry brutally and tragically.

In North America as well, Europeans changed the landscape by introducing foreign plant and animal species. Unable to imagine living without meat, milk, cheese, and butter, English settlers in New England and along the Chesapeake Bay brought European livestock to keep for food. Animal husbandry in Britain had evolved over hundreds—even thousands—of years, ample time for farmers to develop nutritious strains of grass for their animals, but New World plants had evolved independently of Old World animals and were not especially nourishing to them. Back home, these Englishmen had been able to simply let their animals graze and assume they'd get enough to eat close to home, but in Massachusetts and Virginia, the cows and pigs had to feed over a larger area, replacing quality with quantity.

At the same time, the settlers were not in a position to give the animals the same level of care they'd provided back in Europe. They'd come from a land where their farms and gardens were well established; now they were putting down roots in a place where they needed to clear virgin forest and pull boulders out of the soil. They hadn't anticipated this amount of work, and it left them little time to care for their livestock, much less grow special crops dedicated to feeding them. Farmers in the Chesapeake Bay region and Virginia quickly began growing tobacco, lucky to find a product that fetched good money back in Europe. But this endeavor took almost all of their energy, leaving them little time or attention for their pigs and cows.

The indigenous Americans had no domesticated animals, largely because most of the species native to their hemisphere lacked qualities that made them good candidates for forming close ties with humans, unlike the horses, dogs, pigs, and cows of the Eurasian continents. These species tend to be naturally social and inclined to the types of hierarchical relationships which make them congenitally submissive. The Native Americans of the Northeastern United States had names for different animals but, according to European lexicographers who carefully studied their languages, they had no word for "animal" in general. Humans did not occupy a unique and superior place in their cosmos with dominion over all creatures. Instead, they saw themselves as one species among many, each with its particular niche.

As European beasts began to populate their forests, Native Americans naturally hunted them, originally failing to understand that these animals were private property. These unwitting poachers were severely punished by the settlers, who used a version of the British legal system which considered it a grave crime to pilfer another man's livestock. Roaming herds helped themselves to the Indians' carefully tended gardens, causing understandable anger and frustration. The settlers' courts did try to compensate the victims of these incidents—with varying degrees of sincerity—but the presence of livestock in early North American settlements was an ongoing source of friction.

At the same time that Old World animal species were wreaking havoc in the New World, many New World foods circulated in the opposite direction, changing the ways that Europeans, Africans, and Asians ate. Most of our information about the foods of pre-colonial Mexico, which had a particularly profound impact on European diets, came from a Franciscan friar named Bernardino de Sahagun. He meticulously documented the cuisine of the Aztecs, who lived in present-day Mexico. King Phillip of Spain personally faulted the friar, urging him to move on to more important endeavors. Luckily, de Sahagun did not comply. His writings offer a wealth of information about Aztec cooking techniques, as well as the many plants and animals that they used for food and flavoring. He also described Aztec mealtime rites, some of which bear an uncanny resemblance to European customs.

Like the Europeans, the Aztecs had a complicated system of food-related rituals, sanctifying some foods and linking them with reverence and celebration.Like Catholics since medieval times, the Aztecs had a detailed set of fasting conventions, which mostly involved renouncing particular foods for a given length of time, especially salt and chile. These customs clearly had a spiritual dimension and, more than likely, were a way of exploring issues of sacrifice and choice.

Much has been written about Aztec practices of human sacrifice and cannibalism, which were highly ritualized and undoubtedly sacred. It is likely that the westerners who first encountered these practices exaggerated their frequency, in part because they found them exotic and horrifying and also because these portrayals made the Aztecs seem less human and more deserving of the brutal conquest they endured at the hands of the Spaniards. Aztec cannibalism does not seem to have been an everyday occurrence. When they did cook human flesh, the Aztecs cooked it without chile, avoiding the seasoning that they used in most other dishes. This food was different.

Europeans arriving in North and South America could not import all of their provisions and were forced to adapt to eating some local foods. But they accepted these foods on their own terms, with varying degrees of relish. In North and Central America, maize was the primary staple in much the same way that wheat was the basic source of sustenance in Europe at that time. We have come to refer to it as "corn," but before Europeans encountered maize, "corn" was a generic term used for any kind of grain.

Spaniards and Englishmen understood the role that maize played in the diets of Native Americans by relating it to the privileged place of wheat in their own diets. They did feel that it produced inferior bread, an understandable conclusion in light of the fact that Europeans had spent thousands of years selecting strains of wheat that interacted well with yeast, refining and perfecting the product that was so dear to their hearts. Maize couldn't produce satisfying, hard-crusted, yeasted bread, but it had other qualities to recommend it, such as the fact that it yields more calories per acre than any other grain.

Columbus brought maize back with him from his first transatlantic voyage. We don't know much about how corn cultivation spread across Europe, Asia, and Africa, although its cultivation seems to have moved eastward through southern Europe and also southward into Africa before catching on in Northern Europe. The dearth of information suggests that its movement occurred mostly at a grassroots level, like the dissemination of seed stocks since the very beginning of agriculture.

Potatoes, like corn, were brought across the Atlantic by early European explorers and evolved over time into one of the world's most important food crops. They caught on early in Ireland, where they may have washed up on one of the island's beaches with the remnants of a shipwreck. Most of the fertile cropland in Ireland was owned by the English, who used it to grow wheat for export. The typical Irish family during the seventeenth and eighteenth century eked subsistence out of a piece of land smaller than an acre. By planting that plot almost exclusively with potatoes, they could grow enough food to eat for nearly the entire year. The spread of potato agriculture in Ireland led to a population explosion but eventually had a tragic outcome. By covering the entire island with a single subspecies, the Irish left themselves vulnerable to a devastating potato blight during the mid-nineteenth century, which wiped out virtually their entire food supply, causing widespread famine.

In other parts of Europe, potatoes were a hard sell. Governments quickly recognized their potential to alleviate ongoing food shortages, but their citizens were wary. The upper classes were slow to embrace this new food, which they found insipid, so the less affluent scorned them as well. One German monarch wore a potato flower in his buttonhole in an attempt to popularize them. Perhaps the most successful public relations campaign on behalf of the earthy tuber came from a French army pharmacist named Parmentier, who had been fed potatoes when he was a prisoner of war in Germany and quickly recognized their potential to efficiently feed his own countrymen, if they could only be convinced to try them. He persuaded the king to plant a potato garden and surround it with armed guards at night. After a few days, the monarch deliberately stopped protecting the field. The peasants broke in, stole the plants and planted them in their own gardens.

People around the world embraced the chile much more readily than the potato. It offered a flavor similar to the coveted and expensive black pepper that was such an important item in international trade. Unlike black pepper, which only grows in tropical regions, chiles grow in a wide range of temperate climates and are highly adaptable. In fact, today we have varieties of chiles that we associate with parts of the world far from the plant's original home, like the superhot Thai chiles, and the milder, fragrant paprika, which is used so often in Spanish and Hungarian cuisine. Some wealthy Europeans scorned chiles when they first appeared, deriding them as peasant food, but they quickly grew so popular that commerce in black pepper began to decline, striking yet another devastating blow to the Portuguese and Dutch spice trades.

Chocolate, or cacao, was another new world food that enjoyed rapid success in the Old World. It was a high status item for the Aztecs, who used it as currency and also in a wide variety of foods and drinks, both sweet and savory. It was most commonly enjoyed as a hot beverage, especially by Aztec royalty. It was first adopted enthusiastically by the Spanish, in part because the Catholic Church accepted it as a food suitable for fast days. During the seventeenth and eighteenth centuries in Europe, it was commonly associated with decadence, with French paintings from that time portraying elegant women lounging in bed drinking chocolate. Chocolate shops opened in major European cities. Protestant moralists saw these storefronts as havens for illicit activities, but they were mostly just places to gather and savor a flavorful, respectable drink.

It is not surprising that the New World foods that caught on the most easily in Europe could be easily grafted onto the continent's class conceits. Chiles acted as a stand-in for an expensive spice, while chocolate arrived with its own legacy as a food of the elite. Despite the early popularity of these new flavors, the American foods which were to have the greatest impact on the rest of the world were the common staples, especially manioc, corn, and potatoes. Although they were originally greeted with ambivalence and even disdain, they ultimately proved themselves as prolific and important crops, useful enough to transcend long-standing prejudices.

Revolutions in Taste

T HE FIRST COFFEEHOUSE opened in London in 1652, starting a trend which changed the culture of the continent,
along with its eating and drinking habits. Soon similar businesses opened in neighboring countries as well, using the model
of a public gathering place where, for the cost of a hot beverage,
one could linger for stimulating discussions. Proprietors stocked
their shops with current issues of periodicals, turning these spaces into conduits for information and opinions. In an age where
kings ruled by virtue of a divine mandate and many families still
eked out a subsistence living on isolated feudal homesteads, this
new forum for sharing ideas was electrifying.

Europe was slowly modernizing. The economic ideal during the Middle Ages had been self-sufficiency with each manor
striving to meet its own basic needs. This began to shift with
the growth of towns and guilds during the thirteenth and fourteenth centuries and continued changing as the culture and
economy grew more complicated. Fledgling industries drew
an increasing number of people away from the countryside
and into the cities, while new agricultural techniques spurred

landowners to displace long-term tenants in order to efficiently farm larger stretches of land. As the budding entrepreneurial class began centralizing production of commodities and necessities and importing and exporting shiploads of grains, the average person faced food security issues that they hadn't known when they worked small plots of land and tended their own pigs and chickens.

There had been good years and bad years even under the feudal system, but now families faced the added difficulty of price fluctuations, symptoms of a market economy. During years with bad harvests, speculators bought up entire crops, assured of high prices. Often they shipped staple foods to foreign lands, hoping to fetch more money for them overseas. Citizens of coastal towns in France and England watched bushels of wheat being loaded onto ships bound for distant places while they themselves couldn't afford enough bread to feed their families. Food riots grew common as working people reacted to mercenary injustices. These riots weren't eruptions of senseless violence, but rather spontaneous assertions of price control. Sometimes, rather than simply seizing bread from the bakers, crowds took control of inventory and sold the loaves for a cost they deemed fair, turning the proceeds over to the proprietors. But the bakers, like the rioters, were at the mercy of broader markets, raising their prices because their ingredients were growing more expensive.

The widespread discontent that touched off these riots fomented in the era's coffeehouses. As hubs of information and discussion, they shaped public opinion, a phenomenon that was itself in its infancy. The monarchies of the major European territories were engaged in costly, bloody wars that spanned centuries, spending their kingdoms' valuable resources on feuds over territory or their dynasties' succession to neighboring thrones. The common people saw fortunes being squandered while they struggled to survive and shared their frustration with their fellow coffee drinkers.

In France, in particular, the political and economic situation became untenable towards the end of the eighteenth century. Louis XVI drove the country into bankruptcy with his lavish lifestyle and unending foreign wars. The monarch had wholeheartedly continued the traditions of excess which his royal ancestors had enjoyed. He lived in the opulent palace at Versailles, spent his days hunting, and dined off of gold and silver dishes attended by scores of servants, including three whose only function was to fill his water glass. The quality and quantity of the king's dinners was common knowledge. The royal family's daily meals were observed by a ticket-holding audience, who watched every bite of the ritualized proceedings. One only needed to be decently dressed in order to attend.

To address the financial crisis, Louis XVI called a meeting of the Estates General in May 1789. It was the first scheduled meeting in 175 years of the legislative body, which included representatives of the nobility, the clergy, and the "Third Estate," or people who didn't fit into either of these categories. The Third Estate included peasants and craftspeople, and also the bourgeoisie, or those who achieved some measure of wealth by means of their wit and business skills, rather than because of their ancestry. In this pre-Marxist, preindustrial era, the idea of empowering the bourgeoisie rather than the gentry was novel and radical. Their bid for power at the 1789 meeting of the Estates General represented a break from tradition in the sense that it reformed the system to make room for new wealth. But in the sense that it gave a disproportionately large voice to those with money, it was nothing new.

France during that period still clung pathologically to vestiges of the feudal system and the medieval economy, despite the emergence of new ways of thinking and doing business. In the countryside, peasants paid percentages of their income to the lords who controlled the land and also to the church for the safekeeping of their souls. In towns and cities, craftsmen and entrepreneurs faced formidable obstacles establishing themselves in the face of the ossified guild system, which strictly delimited the products and services they could offer to the public. Discontent was rampant.

In addition to the troubles brought about by the monarchy's imprudent spending, the meeting of the Estates General also came on the heels of a series of meteorological disasters, which culminated with the failure of the harvest in 1788. There was a widespread perception in France that the government was conspiring to keep the people hungry by hording stocks of grain and keeping prices artificially high. While this was not necessarily the case, the conspicuous consumption of the royalty and nobility couldn't help but outrage the starving population, creating a climate ripe for tumultuous change.

The Estates General started their meeting by quibbling for several weeks about matters of procedure. Finally, the Third Estate gained the upper hand and declared their determination to write a constitution, changing France from a monarchy into a republic. News of the proceedings trickled out and created mayhem in the streets of Paris. The king resorted to calling up his military, but he changed his mind before the troops reached the capital, fearful that the soldiers would side with the rioters. In response to this threat of violence, the revolutionaries assembled their own army and stormed the Bastille in mid-July, claiming its stockpile of arms. Then they set about reforming the country's infrastructure, seizing valuable church lands and selling them to cover the monstrous national debt and taking steps towards ending the widespread seigniorial obligations, those feudal vestiges which obligated peasants to pay unreasonable fees to landowners.

Because the French have such a strong heritage of eating well, the revolution's metaphors and ideology were often expressed in terms of food. Popular cartoons portrayed the king or the nation as a restaurant patron with a check coming due, an image that represented the national debt, which could no longer be ignored, as well as the monarch's overdue obligation to his people. Restaurants were relatively new institutions and were to evolve considerably during this tumultuous time, paralleling political events. Historians have attributed the rise of the restaurant during the French revolutionary period to widespread unemployment among the chefs who had previously served the dispossessed nobility. But the first restaurants had actually opened in Paris decades prior to the revolution.

The very word "restaurant" originally described a restorative broth, prepared by cooking meat so delicately and thoroughly that only its essence remained, in the form of an easily digestible liquid. Weak chests and fragile constitutions were fashionable among the upper classes and intellectual elite of the time, and the fledgling restaurants could pamper sufferers with food specifically designed to help them heal. They didn't even need to wait for regular mealtimes: they could come in and be served any time their temperamental systems required them to eat. This arrangement was a change from the earlier format for eating a public meal, in which a caterer, or *traiteur*, prepared food and served it at a common table to whoever showed up and paid the price at designated mealtimes. Many members of the upper classes found the food and the company at these establishments

too coarse for their taste and welcomed the new, more refined alternatives.

But restaurants were not strictly for the upper classes. The
only requirement for being able to dine was being able to pay
the price of the food, although coarse behavior and shabby dress
surely caused other diners to look askance. As the revolution
progressed and marks of class and privilege became targets of
moral outrage—not to mention food for the guillotine—this
egalitarian spirit was reflected in the period's restaurants as well.
A wider range of choices appeared on the menus, including hardier fare. The very act of reading through a list of options and
choosing among them was revolutionary in the sense that it was
a symptom of the culture's changing focus from the family or
the community to the individual. Each diner selected his very
own meal, a radical departure from the communal pot of food
served by the *traiteur.*

We can trace the beginnings of the concept of taste to this time.
Just as the coffeehouses provided a forum for individual opinions, restaurants provided their patrons with an environment
suited to finetuning personal preferences. Like the revolution itself, the idea of taste became something of a mirror for a people
in the process of separating themselves from the influence of a
parasitic aristocracy, only to find themselves repressed by different sorts of tyrants and torn by new contradictions.

Though the modern culinary arts evolved in late medieval
and Renaissance kitchens, meals from that time focused more on
sumptuousness than subtlety. Every aspect of these lavish dinners reflected the wealth of the hosts and the social ranking of
the guests, from the sheer number of dishes to the seating chart
and the order in which attendees received their meat. In contrast, the new gastronomic ethic emerging in Paris at the time

of the French Revolution stressed quality and craftsmanship. According to this new ideal, you didn't need to be rich in order to enjoy fine food. You only needed to educate your palate by paying attention to your individual experience, tasting and learning.

The food culture of the period married the emerging scientific consciousness, which saw the world as accessible through a methodical process of inquiry, with the competing emotional worldview expressed by the poets of the Romantic period. Food was a fitting subject for analysis and study, but it was also deeply personal, accessed through the interior world of feeling. Neither of these approaches would have been possible without the intellectual advances of the preceding Age of Enlightenment when the people started to find their voice, questioning the divine mandate of their kings and the church's self-proclaimed monopoly on moral authority. Now that these institutions no longer dictated laws and opinions, the world was ripe for discovery by rigorous observation as well as personal experience. Independent restaurateurs could experiment with new dishes, and enquiring eaters could sample them and select their favorites.

This new way of seeing the world and experiencing one's food was liberating for cooks and their patrons, but it was hardly as egalitarian as it seemed on the surface. You didn't need to belong to a certain class in order to eat in a restaurant, but you did need to afford to pay for your meal, a requirement that screened many potential customers. Anyone could learn to tell the difference between good food and bad, but preparing good food often requires time, skill, and care, which make it more expensive than offerings of lower quality.

The ability to taste the difference between good food and its mediocre alternatives required a culinary education of sorts, which brewed its own variety of snobbery. We can trace the origins of restaurant criticism to this time. The famous gastronome Grimod de Reyneire wrote the first restaurant guidebooks during the 1790s, sampling humble and elegant fare all over Paris and making recommendations about everything from bread and pastry to ham and foie gras. Anyone could sample food and form opinions about it, but now experts were emerging, whose impressions could guide the tastes of others.

In a country where eating well was a firmly established value, it was fitting that the newly established revolutionary government chose to express the newfound solidarity and equality of her citizens by hosting communal meals. An important part of the revolution's historical legacy was the modern idea of the nation, or a group of people with an identity held in common, as opposed to the medieval idea of a state controlled by a monarch whose right to the throne was divinely ordained and passed on within a hereditary lineage. The people of France were eager to define themselves in ways that were uniquely French, and they found much of their inspiration in the world of food.

The communal meals shared by French citizens during Jacobin times were not lavish events, but they did involve sharing bread and wine, two foodstuffs that were essential to everyday meals. Both symbolized basic food as well as an inviolable right to eat well. Either could come in the form of subsistence fare or a fine artisan product. In the early, heady days after the birth of the republic, activists speculated that true liberty, equality, and fraternity could be achieved if all of Paris dined together in the streets. In July of 1790 to celebrate the birth of the republic, Louis XVI planned just such a meal. Speculation and debate raged during the weeks leading up to the feast. If this was an event designed for everyone to dine together, then who would cook and serve the meal? If some people were cooking and serving while others were dining, how could the event be truly egalitarian?

It is significant that this public discourse even existed. It indicates, as we have already seen, that food served as a metaphor for the many ideas and changes that were taking place at the time. And it shows us, once again, how seriously the French people took their meals. These debates and changing attitudes towards food paralleled every step of this tumultuous time. During the Terror when every sign of opulence was suspect—and even dangerous—restaurateurs referred to themselves as "humble *traiteurs*." During the spring and summer of 1794, Paris neighborhoods regularly held fraternal banquets in the streets with everyone contributing what they could. This potluck format solved the problem of having some people serving at an event where everyone was supposed to be equal. Their concern now was to choose an offering that made them seem neither too stingy nor too affluent.

Later, during Napoleonic times, the weighty issues that had precipitated the revolution were pushed to the back burner. The nation breathed a collective sigh of relief, and the new restaurants truly thrived. Despite the ongoing foreign wars and Napoleon's own legendary indifference to food , the restaurant culture of Paris now came into its own as a venue where creative artisans could innovate, and passionate patrons could enjoy their output. Before the revolution, the rigid guild structure had strictly limited what any producer could make and sell. There were clear lines between *traiteurs*, the caterers who served meals at a common table, and restaurateurs, who offered their customers a choice of foods. During the years preceding the revolution, a restaurateur could even find himself in legal trouble for offering a ragout, or stew, rather than the simple broth that his establishment was licensed to offer. Many food service entrepreneurs defined themselves with hyphenated titles which allowed them to practice different culinary arts together. This was necessary for as simple an enterprise as preparing a meat pie that was served in a pastry shell because this dish required the skills of both the pastry cook and the meat cook.

These limitations grew considerably more relaxed during the 1790s as the revolution disassembled many of the antiquated remnants of medieval life. As the Reign of Terror ended and Napoleon eventually came to power, the citizens of Paris were eager to enjoy basic daily pleasures. Napoleon himself understood that allowing the population to distract themselves would lessen the potential for civil unrest. The climate was ripe for cooks to strike out on their own and innovate, feeding the growing entrepreneurial middle class.

Not all of these cooks worked in restaurants. The most famous French chef of the post-revolutionary period, Antonin Careme, came into his own as a pastry chef. As a homeless urchin, he was taken in by the owner of a chop house, who taught him how to make soup, and later he began an apprenticeship with a *patissier* on the rue Vivienne, where he learned to create delicacies from spun sugar. He became an expert in this medieval art, even studying classical architecture and using his sweet medium to create replicas of ancient buildings. Like Napoleon himself who rose from humble beginnings to eventually be crowned emperor, Careme rose in the world of food by sheer virtue of his talent. These meteoric paths to power and fame would not have been possible even fifty years earlier, when only sons of nobles could earn commissions in the army, and craftsmen had to labor for years under the constraints of the antiquated guild system before being allowed to strike out on their own.

At a time when many French chefs were founding restaurants after leaving positions with wealthy households, Careme left the world of culinary commerce to cook privately for some of the most powerful statesmen of his time, men of deep pockets and profound appreciation for food. Not all of his employers were French: they included Tsar Alexander I of Russia and England's charismatic Lord Stewart, as well as the Duke of Wellington. His final—and happiest—position was with the French banker Jacob Rothchild, a phenomenally wealthy and successful man who was having difficulty breaking into the world of French high society. He was Jewish, and his wealth was newly acquired, two facts that shouldn't have counted against him in post-revolutionary Paris, but some old prejudices endured. His luck only turned once he hired the eminent chef. Now all of Paris coveted invitations to the elegant dinners that he hosted several times a week. In a fascinating reversal of a traditional dynamic, the prestige and talent of the employee conferred respect on the employer.

While Careme was preparing elaborate banquets to be served in the mansions of the capital, the peasants in the countryside were adapting to the aftermath of the revolution. They had been freed from paying many of the tithes and seigniorial obligations that had burdened their class for centuries, but they had also lost many of the benefits that came along with these feudal relationships. They could no longer graze their animals in the lord's woodlands or grind their grain in his mill.

In other countries across Europe, the end of medieval landholding relationships led to the concentration of property in the hands of the new entrepreneurial class, who treated it as an asset to be developed and milked for profit, in the spirit of the emerging Industrial Revolution. But the recent history of France stood in the way of such economies of scale. Her attention was focused elsewhere, first on building a new kind of state, and later on the military feats of Napoleon. Unlike Britain where the government helped to create an efficient economic machine, the ongoing upheaval and turmoil in post-revolutionary France stood in the way of consolidation and industrialization.

For this reason, France remained one of the only countries in Europe where small-scale agriculture has survived into modern times as a viable institution. Just as conditions in ancient Greece enabled a class of free landowners to stand on their own and develop a collective identity with democratic institutions, in France many independent farmers have been able to hold onto plots and keep them in their families for many generations. It is no accident that the French countryside produces such fine wine and olive oil, the same products that built the legacy of ancient rural Greece. As we have seen, grapevines and olive trees take special care to grow, requiring the kind of expertise that can only be developed over time as farmers get to know the strengths and idiosyncrasies of their own soil. They can also be transformed into artisan products, using skills that are most likely to develop among independent operators. There is a long list of foods produced in France that also fit into this category, from two hundred and fifty plus varieties of cheese, to breads, sausages, and pates.

The genius of French food since the French Revolution has been its capacity to unite the bourgeois emphasis on practiced technique and discriminating taste with the rural artisan tradition of working independently to bring out the best of what available raw materials have to offer. There have certainly been periods during the intervening years when artifice has taken the upper hand over honest, well-crafted food, such as the nineteenth century focus on rich sauces. But over time this venerable cooking tradition has always cycled back around to the solid historical foundation which has made it the role model for many contemporary chefs working to revive our fundamental respect for food.

NOTHING WAS MORE antithetical to this spirit of gastronomical artistry than the food system evolving contemporaneously in nearby Britain, the birthplace of the Industrial Revolution. Unlike France where the king's power and even his claim to divinely sanctioned rule endured until late in the eighteenth century, the British had beheaded a monarch in 1649. Subsequent governments, though still under the leadership of a king, reflected a broader base of power. Parliament now included entrepreneurs as well as hereditary gentry, and it often legislated on behalf of business interests. This political climate was ripe for innovative enterprise by a class whose agenda was at odds with the small-scale farmers who had traditionally peopled the English countryside.

The first victims of the new industrial economy were the agricultural laborers, workers who farmed for wages on large estates. They did not own land themselves, but many of them leased cottages on small plots, growing much of their own food and raising a head or two of livestock, which grazed on public lands known as the commons. As affluent landowners began experimenting with modern agricultural techniques, they increasingly appropriated these collective grazing areas by issuing parliamentary mandates known as "enclosure acts," named for the fact that the parcels were now fenced for private use. With no available land to raise their pigs and cows, workers found it increasingly difficult to feed their families. Many of these displaced laborers moved to the towns and found jobs in the newly built factories or sewed and weaved in their own homes, getting paid by the piece.

Britain's emerging industrial economy was based on her unique position as a colonial empire controlling territories all over the globe. These foreign lands provided products that British businesses could sell to British citizens, and the inhabitants of the colonies were also potential markets for goods manufactured at home. British laborers could buy tea grown in China and India, and sugar produced on the empire's Caribbean islands. They wove cotton from India and the southern United States, and the garments they made were then exported back to the Americas and also to Africa, where they could be traded for the slaves that made up most of workforce harvesting sugar and cotton in the colonies.

The industrial workers in England, like the inhabitants of the colonies, were cogs in the machine that produced heaps of marketable stuff. They were also potential buyers of factory products from home and colonial goods from overseas. Agricultural workers had traditionally received some compensation in the form of food in addition to the wages they earned, and they could also eat the vegetables they grew in their gardens and the livestock they raised themselves. They weaved some of their own clothes from available wool and flax, made soap from tallow, hats from straw, and beer from barley. Virtually all of these resources and skills were lost when they moved to urban areas and leased rooms in dingy flats. Now they needed to spend cash money on practically all of their household needs.

Their diets declined considerably as they lost the diversity of foods they'd produced in their own kitchen gardens and the wild plants they'd gathered from nearby wooded areas. Now they had considerably less variety to eat, but they were able to enjoy foods that they hadn't previously been able to afford. They earned barely enough to make ends meet, but the genius of the empire created economies of scale sufficient to lower the price on many products that had once been luxuries available only to the very wealthy. Sugar, in particular, changed over the centuries from an expensive condiment and medicinal ingredient, an emblem of conspicuous consumption, to a fundamental source of calories for the working poor.

During the early years of this transition, it must have been exciting for these budding consumers to be able to afford it, and it kept some whisper of its special status for generations. In fact, the idea of sweetness carries remnants of its former mystique even until today, being a metaphor for goodness in general, such as when we refer to a kind deed as sweet. To be sure, there is an evolutionary, biological component to our predilection for sweetness: it is a flavor that we are naturally predisposed to enjoy, an indication that fruit is ripe. But there are also countless layers of sociocultural associations heaped on top of this physical inclination.

Despite the pleasure that it offers to our palates, sugar has generated more bitterness and sorrow than perhaps any other food crop. It was the original catalyst for the transatlantic slave trade, which later manned the cotton plantations in the southern United States as well. The Portuguese, French, Dutch, and English all relied on slave labor to process their sugar crops, but by the end of the eighteenth century, the English dominated the trade, importing virtually all of the sugar they grew in their colonies to feed burgeoning demand at home. The technology for refining sugar at the time produced a variety of grades with different degrees of purity through a process of boiling raw materials and treating them with chemicals to remove everything except the pure sucrose. Molasses that was separated during the purification process was used to make rum, a profitable by-product that was especially popular with the British navy. The whitest grades, which had been most thoroughly processed, were naturally the most expensive and were consumed largely by the wealthy classes, while poorer folk mostly used "clayed" sugar, a less pure and cheaper variety, or treacle, a golden syrup that was also less refined.

As production techniques grew more efficient and the price of sugar dropped, Britain's urban poor found new ways of incorporating it into their diet. Per capita consumption rose from four pounds in 1700 to fifty pounds by 1850, and by 1900, one sixth of all calories consumed by the British working class came from sugar. Its new uses paralleled changing living conditions as families moved from rural cottages to urban flats. Purchases of tea, the emerging national beverage, went hand in hand with sugar production. Like sugar, tea was a product of the colonial empire, grown in China and India, and it started out as a luxury consumed mainly by the wealthier classes. Its potential for generating profit spurred the British government and the entrepreneurs it represented to build an infrastructure capable of producing and importing quantities ample enough to drive the price down until nearly everyone could afford it, if only in the form of weak brews from reused tea leaves.

In addition to its impressive capacity for generating capital for the entrepreneurial class, tea fit well into the emerging industrial economy because it provided workers with something warm to drink when they had neither the time nor the equipment to prepare a filling hot meal. Sweetened amply with sugar, tea could also be a source of calories. Workers could drink it during breaks and have it for dinner along with the bread and jam, which also became dietary staples during this period.

The practice of preserving fruit with sugar dated back many centuries; in fact, Arab traders had imported sugared fruit into

Europe since early medieval times. Candying fruit served the dual function of extending its shelf life so it could survive the long journey from the Middle East and also transforming it into a product that medieval consumers felt was more digestible. Needless to say, only the rich could afford it, at least at that point. As sugar became more affordable during the eighteenth and nineteenth centuries, jam became a working class food. Unlike the sugared, imported fruits of medieval times, the jam of the industrial age contained more sugar than fruit. But it could be stored at room temperature and quickly made into a meal, two features which made it indispensable to nineteenth-century British factory workers.

At the same time that British entrepreneurs were developing the infrastructure to cheaply import tea and sugar, rural landowners were developing economies of scale that enabled them to mass produce beef, lowering its price. Enjoyment of beef was already an integral part of the British national identity by the seventeenth and eighteenth centuries. Cartoons from Napoleonic times depicted a big, healthy Englishman facing up against an emaciated Frenchman, implying that the British predilection for beef made her people bigger and manlier than their neighbors across the channel. The same Enclosure Acts that made small-scale husbandry impractical by appropriating shared grazing areas ironically worked to enable displaced homesteaders to eat meat on a more regular basis, even if it didn't come from their own animals.

In addition to fencing common areas, the emerging beef industry consolidated strips of land which had previously been leased to individual households through a system known as "furlong." With access to larger plots, rural entrepreneurs could graze larger herds. They dedicated grain crops specifically to the purpose of feeding their livestock, bulking the animals up quickly, and producing a rich, fatty texture known as "marbling," which suited the tastes of their customers. Back when the English landscape had been peopled by cottagers who produced most of their own food, the average family kept a couple of barnyard animals. They fattened their pigs on scraps through the spring and summer and allowed them to forage in nearby wooded areas. Then they slaughtered them in the fall and enjoyed a bounty of fresh meat for a short period, preserving the rest as ham and bacon to be eaten sparingly throughout the rest of the year. With the growth of the beef industry and the population shift from the country to the towns, meat became a year-round staple, rather than a seasonal treat.

The price fell, especially for the cheaper cuts which the wealthier classes didn't want. Trotters, or pig's feet, were a favorite among the British working classes, who had previously only enjoyed them seasonally. The construction of roads, canals, and railroads brought meat to the cities more quickly and efficiently than ever. British entrepreneurs also invested heavily in the development of the American West and the Argentinean cattle industry where—once the buffalo and Native American tribes had been cleared away—livestock could graze in areas whose scope had been previously unimaginable in Europe. The invention of refrigeration in the mid-nineteenth century helped the meat industry to become even more cost effective. Product could be stored in larger quantities for longer periods of time. Fish became a staple working-class food as well, now that it could be shipped to cities before it spoiled.

The British working classes drank weak tea and sweetened it with sugar whose price had dropped until it was their most cost-effective source of calories. They ate cheap cuts of meat prepared in ways that stretched the available supply, like meat pies which contained at least as much pastry as beef or pork. They ate their fish battered and fried, a cooking technique that was well suited to disguising spoiled pieces. Yet all of these foods retained a trace of their former luster, offering bright spots in the midst of a grueling workweek. The mass production of meat was especially effective in bringing solace to the overworked, underpaid urban dwellers fueling the early industrial machine. The allure of sugar, tea, and white bread reached back hundreds of years, but the special status of meat was older than civilization, dating back at least as far as the Paleolithic hunt.

The reverence for food that flourished across the channel during the years following the French Revolution was dramatically different from the proliferation of cheap convenience products taking place simultaneously in England. But these two developments shared an emphasis on individual choice or taste. As we have seen, the many options laid out on the printed menus of Paris restaurants for the first time gave diners the experience of selecting dishes that suited their fragile constitutions. The street foods of London didn't offer anything remotely resembling this sense of luxury, but they did provide a degree of choice that was equally novel in the world of food.

The very fact that these early industrial workers could exchange a neutral commodity—money—for products that could offer them nourishment and pleasure hailed the arrival of a new era, when the average person's diet was no longer limited by what grew in his immediate vicinity during any given time of year. In the cities, neighborhood shops began stocking a greater variety of items including different blends of tea, multiple brands of biscuits, and countless varieties of catsup, the national condiment.

These simple, everyday choices provided some sense of autonomy and control in the face of a daily existence where so much was rigid and predetermined. For better or for worse, we started down the road to becoming consumers.

The Great American Dyspepsia

For Europeans settlers, America was a land of plenty. The woods teemed with game, and the skies flew thick with birds. An enterprising homesteader could claim a plot of land and patiently build a legacy, regardless of his origins. But there were real hardships. Familiar crops and livestock didn't immediately thrive in the foreign landscape. Rocks and trees needed to be uprooted to prepare fields for planting. These tasks often took longer than a growing season, leaving a farmer with little to eat over the first winter. To make matters worse, familiar crops and animals didn't easily take to this unfamiliar landscape. The settlers craved bread and beef rather than corn, squash, and venison.

Out of necessity, they adapted. At first they relied heavily on wild game because it was plentiful and because it was a lot less work to track and shoot a deer than to clear and plow a field, sow seeds, weed the area, wait for plants to grow, and finally harvest them. Initially, the act of hunting must have been strange and exciting for the colonists, many of whom came from lands where only royalty were traditionally allowed to hunt; in fact, in some European countries, poaching was a capital offense.

The pig was the first domesticated animal successfully introduced to North America. It could forage in the woods or eat the corn that was already abundant before the Revolutionary War. Pork could be salted and preserved, rendering it available throughout the winter when it could be added to almost any dish, at any meal. Sailors, soldiers, and explorers carried it on journeys. Salt pork became a symbol of the rough hardiness of the American spirit. One group of early American loggers complained when their employer splurged on fresh beef, grumbling that they wouldn't have the energy to work after eating such fancy food.

Settlers developed food-related industries, sending salted cod across the Atlantic and shipping heads of cattle to the British Isles. A hardy class of independent farmers amply provisioned their families on their own land as the new nation expanded westward. Early American cookbooks call for quantities that seem staggering today, like cakes containing thirty eggs and stews containing six pounds of beef. These concoctions were probably intended to feed tables of ravenous farmhands, but they're not the kinds of recipes that you prepare when food is scarce.

Both George Washington and Thomas Jefferson were skilled, innovative farmers, and the legislation they helped shape as they founded the country recognized the importance of small-scale agriculture in building a healthy economy. Jefferson wrote repeatedly of the social and economic significance of widespread land ownership, recognizing the historical correlation between a strong, independent middle class and a healthy central government. Several generations later, Justin Morrill, a senator from

Vermont, sponsored legislation authorizing a system of colleges throughout the country geared towards teaching and improving American agriculture. Although these Land Grant institutions have lately played a central role in the industrialization of farming, their original intention was very much in the spirit of Jefferson's ideal of building a population of skilled and knowledgeable independent horticulturalists.

The history of the United States is the story of the tension between this ethic of broad-based wealth and the aggressive lobbying of wealthy businessmen molding government policy to meet their own needs. This dynamic started almost immediately after the Revolutionary War as the banks, acting in the interests of the wealthy, created conditions ripe for large-scale landowners to increase their holdings at the expense of small operators. Because of a shortage of paper money, many small-scale farmers could not come by enough currency to pay their debts and lost their land. Shay's Rebellion of 1780 was an uprising of farmers protesting the government's refusal to print extra money on their behalf.

Despite the independent spirit that was such a vital part of the fledgling nation's identity, the system of land ownership in place in some states at the time of the American Revolution looked suspiciously like the feudal system, which even European nations were outgrowing. Eighty families owned almost all of the land in upstate New York, renting out parcels on terms which assured that their lessees would never become land owners themselves. Less fortunate people weren't even able to secure rental plots and became wage laborers. This exploitative system, like its precursor in Europe, was profitable for land owners in the short term but ultimately stifled the kind of agricultural innovation that would have brought about more broad-based prosperity. A series of renters' rebellions in the early nineteenth century eventually led to legislation that transferred some ownership into the hands of the people who actually farmed.

As settlers spread to the western part of the country, Congress passed the Homestead Act of 1830, allocating plots of one hundred and sixty acres to anyone willing and able to farm. After the dissolution of slavery, the government again promised tracts, "forty acres and a mule," to freed slaves establishing themselves as autonomous citizens. Simultaneously, as in Europe, wealthy American entrepreneurs used every possible opportunity to grab property from individual farmers. Entrepreneurs with considerable landholdings achieved economies of scale, enabling them to lower prices and drive smaller competitors out of business. New agricultural innovations such as John Deere's tractor exponentially increased output, but they cost money. Small-scale independent farmers could either continue to farm inefficiently using traditional methods, or they could borrow against the value of their land in order to modernize, at the risk of losing their property to creditors.

With so much available space, it was only natural that these farmers, so heavily influenced by Britain, would raise beef. American herds were descended in part from cattle brought over by Spanish explorers during the sixteenth and seventeenth centuries. The Spaniards lost track of many of their animals, and the livestock grew increasingly feral, adapting to the dry conditions of the Mexican and American southwest regions. These wild herds were eventually bred with heirloom British stock to create varieties especially well suited for their new environment, such as the Texas longhorn.

All that remained to establish a thriving beef industry was to clear the prairie and plains of buffalo, which roamed throughout the areas best suited for grazing livestock. The government offered bounties for killing the animals, whose carcasses littered the landscape during the middle years of the nineteenth century. The railroads wanted them gone as well because they got in the way of high speed transport and because their hides could be profitably shipped back east. Millions of animals were slaughtered, even shot from trains. Before this systematic extermination, there had been at least sixty million buffalo in the region; in fact, no large mammal had ever proliferated as successfully in any other part of the world.

It took less than a century to drive them to the point of extinction. In addition to making room for vast herds of cattle, the holocaust of the buffalo was also a strategy for waging war against the Native American populations that relied on the animal for sustenance, using it for everything from food, to clothing, to tools, to shelter. Aside from the tangible benefits that it provided, the buffalo was an important cultural symbol, a friend and an ally. The buffalo remains a symbol of the Plains tribes' struggle to endure and preserve their age-old ways, playing a central role in the mythology foretelling the end of European domination.

The extermination of the buffalo cleared the way for the growth of a massive beef trade. British entrepreneurs invested heavily, hoping to satisfy their countrymen's insatiable hunger for meat. American cattlemen also worked to meet the needs of the growing cities in the eastern half of the country. Chicago, in particular, was known for its massive stockyards, and even New York City was home to a thriving beef industry during the nineteenth century.

Although Americans had eaten plenty of meat since their earliest days on the continent—especially compared to the Europeans—the growth of the railroads enabled them to consume great quantities of beef in addition to the pork that was already abundant and the venison that had been a staple during colonial days. Cowboys drove great herds from Texas and Wyoming to be loaded onto cattle cars and shipped to Chicago where they could be slaughtered and processed. This new method of transportation enabled a greater number of animals to be transported more quickly, with less danger from weather and disease. The Chicago stockyards achieved unprecedented economies of scale, although they often did so by compromising quality in dangerous ways, as Upton Sinclair described in his 1906 muckraking novel, *The Jungle*.

The profitable, consolidated beef industry, like the railroads, was symptomatic of the economic model that came into its own with the Industrial Revolution, as substantial inputs of capital yielded enormous profits and made it difficult for small-scale operators to compete. The synergy and symbiosis between the two industries was no accident: both were made possible by the kind of entrepreneurial spirit which was relentlessly exploring the limits and possibilities of building tremendous, monopolistic enterprises. Both endeavors also benefited substantially from government policies aimed at opening up the west and encouraging commerce.

During the Lincoln administration, Congress gave 100 million acres of western land to the railroad companies and also to private citizens looking to strike out on their own. Despite the opportunities offered to independent farmers by the Homestead Act, the 160-acre parcels weren't exactly free, but rather were available for the cost of $1.25 an acre. That was a small price to pay for arable land, but it was more than most ordinary citizens could afford. The railroads sponsored sham homesteaders to lay title to claims, especially in the choicest areas closest to tracks and towns. This enabled the cunning entrepreneurs to lay the groundwork for industries that could profitably bring food to the eastern cities.

At first the railroad companies invested their own capital building stockyards in strategic towns along their routes to hold animals which cowboys drove to these depots. By the 1860s, the meatpacking companies were innovating with technologies for mobile cold storage. The usable meat on most livestock makes up only about a third of their weight, so the meat companies could save considerable sums by slaughtering and processing the animals out west, rather them shipping them live to eastern facilities. These new technologies put the meat packers in competition with the railroad barons, who made more money shipping live animals. Ultimately, the meat producers ended up building their own refrigerated cars. The meatpackers also invested heavily in fruit and vegetable production in the west in order to move more goods on their impressive infrastructure. They eventually controlled the lion's share of the nation's food supply.

These developments provided cheap, abundant food for the urban consumer as well as staggering profits for the food conglomerates. As new waves of immigrants came from Europe during the late nineteenth century, the novelty of a plentiful meat supply impressed one generation after another and took the edge off a life of long work hours and cramped tenements. Letters from new arrivals to family back in the old country repeatedly speak of the harsh living conditions but mention the easy availability of meat as an antidote. Cheap meat offered an affordable luxury, an incentive to go to work and adapt to the ways of this foreign land where they were often treated as an intruding underclass. Reformers from this period who tried to work with poor populations and teach them to effectively budget their food dollars regularly complained about the tendency of the urban poor to splurge on cuts of meat, rather than subsisting on cheaper fare, such as salt pork and beans.

American entrepreneurs were able to take the industrialization of the food supply to a new level, feeding millions of people cheaply and profitably and creating the illusion of eating well for many consumers who enjoyed few other luxuries. But the American way of eating came with a price for both the consumers, whose health suffered, and also for the land, which grew depleted and eroded. Complaints of dyspepsia, or indigestion, were common, and it was no wonder: imagine eating a breakfast every day of bread, bacon, eggs, potatoes, and corncakes, and lunches and dinners that were just as substantial. It was a diet suited for farmhands and builders, but an increasing percentage of the population was no longer engaged in physical work. Despite its widely recognized dangers, the trend of overeating continued throughout the nineteenth century and endures to this day with traditions like all-you-can-eat buffets and contests to see who can consume the most pies or hot dogs.

Perhaps the most famous American overeater was "Diamond Jim" Brady, who made his fortune selling heavy equipment to railroad companies and was determinedly spending it on six tremendous meals a day (along with the expensive jewelry which earned him his nickname.) He alternately frequented Delmonico's, New York's most prestigious eatery, as well as less reputable establishments such as Rector's, which catered largely to chorus girls and railroad men. Brady kept company with the actress Lillian Russell, who was regarded as the world's most beautiful woman despite the fact that she could supposedly match Brady bite for bite. George Rector referred to the pair as his "twenty-five best customers." One legend about Brady held that he situated himself four inches from the table when he began each meal, and when his belly expanded enough to touch the table, he knew he'd had enough. He started his dinners with a gallon of orange juice and six dozen oysters. He preferred Lynnhaven oysters, a choice true to his reputation as the quintessential American glutton: oyster connoisseurs consider this variety to be bland, their most notable quality being that they are large. When Brady died of digestive troubles at the age of fifty-six, his stomach was found to be six times the normal size.

No doubt some of these descriptions of Diamond Jim's excesses were grotesque caricatures. Oscar Tschirky, famous head waiter at the Waldorf Astoria, who began his career at Delmonico's, recounted in his memoirs that Brady actually ate far less than one would expect in light of his reputation, but it is possible that Tschirky observed Brady eating during a period when the latter was trying to slim down. Regardless of whether or not these accounts of his mighty appetite are all literally true, the fact that they were circulating and have even endured to this day is typical of a culture that glorifies the consumption of tremendous quantities of food.

It was only natural that there would be a backlash against this type of eating. If Tschirky's account is accurate, even Diamond Jim himself at some point came to the realization that his pace of consumption was unsustainable. For one thing, dyspepsia was its constant companion. Workers were going hungry at the same time that the wealthy socialite was eating many times his share, although Diamond Jim himself probably wasn't much concerned with this fact. Despite the natural abundance that made excess the hallmark of American eating, even this bountiful land was starting to see the limits of its capacity. Settlement had reached the western edge of the land. The supply of the very oysters that

Brady enjoyed so lavishly had been dwindling in the harbors of New York for over a century, causing entrepreneurs to develop techniques for artificially replacing them, with mixed results.

The backlash against American overeating grew out of a need for improving the nation's physical health, but it had a spiritual dimension as well: it represented a quest for something more meaningful than the superficial pleasure of hearty dining. Not surprisingly, some of the earliest critics of the American diet were religious figures who linked the collective passion for large quantities of food with an undue emphasis on worldly matters. For them, abstemiousness was not only a way to maintain a healthy body but also a path to a fit soul.

During the 1830s and 1840s, a Presbyterian minister named Sylvester Graham drew crowds across the country preaching about the evils of the contemporary diet and advocating more austere fare instead. Best remembered for promoting a whole grain product that has survived to this day as the graham cracker, the minister spoke in favor of a vegetarian diet featuring unrefined grains, especially dense, whole wheat bread. By choosing white bread as a symbol of everything that was wrong with American eating, he pitted himself against a food with deep cultural significance. As we have seen, bread was regarded as a special—even sacred—food since ancient Egyptian times, and shortages were cause for social unrest, even helping to precipitate the French Revolution.

Wheat bread, in particular, had historically been a symbol of living well. Wheat required more land and attention than heartier grains such as barley and rye. The process of refining flour was labor intensive and expensive, although techniques were already growing more efficient by Graham's time, making whiter bread available to poorer people. Although struggling families could now afford bread made from refined flour, white bread retained some of its status as a special food. In some sense, Graham's crusade against it was not only a campaign to educate people about the health benefits of the bran and fiber that was being removed from the flour but also a stand against a preoccupation with social status, and the foods that went with it.

Despite Graham's focus on an abstemious diet as a path to spiritual redemption, he was also concerned with the fitness of the body and hoped to live to be one hundred. (He made it to the age of fifty seven.) He exercised rigorously and urged his followers to do the same. But he was a controversial figure and the butt of countless jokes. Newspaper editorials around the country poked fun at him. One Boston meeting where he was supposed to preside degenerated into a brawl between the "Grahamites" and a mob of bakers and butchers who saw him as a threat to their livelihood.

Why did the preacher incite such heated responses? He certainly leveled his criticisms at an essential part of the American identity. Immigrant families clearly remembered a time when they did not have enough to eat or, at the very least, couldn't enjoy meat on a regular basis. Graham also touched the same nerve as members of early Christian sects, who taught that the soul was pure and the body was evil. These teachings were more than mere ideas: they were expressions of values that touched every aspect of how one lived.

During the middle years of the nineteenth century, the most famous American proponent of the ideal of abstemiousness was Ellen White, founder of the Seventh-day Adventist religious sect. The Adventists believed in the imminent end of the world, followed by a sojourn in the kingdom of heaven. They even set a date and waited and, when the world continued as usual, they picked another date. Like Graham, White advocated a vegetarian diet with an emphasis on whole, unprocessed food. She saw separation from worldly pleasures as a way to prepare oneself for the afterlife. These dietary strictures, which came to "Sister White" in a vision, included using a minimum of salt and refraining from spices altogether. Surely this was not only a matter of physical health but also of eschewing any kind of enjoyment that could be had through the senses.

The Adventists founded a health center in their home base of Battle Creek, Michigan, a place where patients could heal the damage that modern living inflicted on their bodies by exercising, eating simply, and taking "water cures," which were in vogue at the time. Looking for a talented doctor to head the institution, the leaders of the sect placed their hopes in a promising young man named John Harvey Kellogg, who came from an Adventist family. They sponsored his medical school education in New York, and when he returned, they placed him in charge of their facility.

The health center thrived under his leadership. He renamed it the Sanitarium, or "San," upgrading its rooms and treatment spaces and assembling a well-trained staff. He was at once extravagant and frugal, dreaming and building on a magnificent scale, yet walking away from potentially lucrative deals when he couldn't acquire a new product or piece of equipment at a rock bottom price. He was a skilled physician, performing surgeries that left small, neat scars that other doctors recognized immediately, referring to them as his signature. And yet many of the treatments he advocated smack of quackery. Patients trying to lose weight lay on tables with sandbags weighting their bellies to aid digestion. Sufferers from heart disease ate grapes, up to fifteen pounds a day.

Kellogg had a genius for marketing, and his reputation grew. He wrote prolifically, publishing tomes and articles. Socialites from all over the country travelled to his facility to "take the cure." Over the years, his Sanitarium attracted such well-known patients as William and Henry James, John D. Rockefeller, and Theodore Roosevelt. Part of Kellogg's success no doubt came from his ability to temper the austerity of his health recommendations with an atmosphere of luxury. Patients might be eating many of the same foods as European peasants, but they did so in a state of the art facility, surrounded by society's elite, with an orchestra entertaining them at mealtimes.

Kellogg inevitably had a falling out with the Adventists, who were troubled by the worldly crowd he was attracting. The success of the institution changed the character of their small town, making it a busy place with a wealth of secular spin-off businesses. Ellen White had visions of a sword dangling over the Sanitarium and of the place in flames. The facility did, in fact, burn several times during the early years of the twentieth century, and there were rumors that the Adventists set the fires. The break between Kellogg and his former teacher was slow and painful. The sect had invested heavily in founding the Sanitarium. Eventually, Kellogg restructured the institution's finances so that it was completely philanthropic and non-sectarian, and the break with his former sponsors was complete.

John Harvey Kellogg had a laboratory at the San devoted to food experiments, where he worked closely with his wife, Ella. They invented foods that we still eat today, including peanut butter and a version of granola, originally called "granula." They introduced meat substitutes such as "protose" and "nutose," which figured prominently in the menus at the facility's elegant dining room. Some of these concoctions today seem comical; in fact, T.C . Boyle lampooned them in his 1994 novel *The Road to Wellville*, which actually derived its name from an advertising slogan used by Kellogg's rival and nemesis, C.W. Post.

Today we know the Kellogg name mainly as a brand on a cereal box, although the Kellogg responsible for popularizing their brand of breakfast cereals was John Harvey's younger brother Will. John Harvey Kellogg did change the way America ate breakfast, lobbying for a light early meal of grains, rather than starting the day with a feast of eggs and meat. He experimented for many years before coming up with a successful technology for transforming grains into an easily digestible, shelf-stable product that could be used as a breakfast cereal. The process for "flaking" grains involves soaking them to soften them and then pressing them through rollers to produce a flake-like shape before drying them so they could be stored in the form of a ready to eat cereal that could be eaten with milk. Kellogg's first successful innovation of this type was a variety of flaked wheat which he began producing commercially in a converted barn behind the Sanitarium in 1895. During the same period, he travelled to Colorado to meet with a businessman and inventor named Henry Perky, who had developed a product made of stretched tendrils of wheat called "shredded wheat." Kellogg was interested in the patent for this new breakfast food but failed to offer Perky an attractive enough price for it.

The most successful breakfast cereal entrepreneur of this period was a former San patient named C.W. Post, who left the institution after finding that its remedies did little to improve his chronic stomach ailments. He set up a rival facility across town, healing clients primarily through a process of positive thinking, rather than physical cures. His first successful product was a grain beverage called Postum, based on a similar concoction that was served at breakfast time at the San as an alternative to coffee. Post did approach Kellogg at one point proposing a collaboration, but the doctor wasn't interested in joining forces with an unknown businessman with few resources.

Postum turned out to be a fantastically successful product, in part because of Post's genius for advertising and his willingness to invest everything he had in promoting his offerings. One ad, which first ran in a Chicago newspaper, showed a red bull's eye and read "It makes red blood." For the modern day consumer, it seems incredible—or at least unspeakably quaint—that consumers would respond to such a claim. Nonetheless, the ad promised vitality, and it made customers want the product.

One advertising company in Chicago was so impressed with the copy that they agreed to underwrite an extensive ad campaign, allowing Post to pay over time. These magazine and newspaper spots were the forerunners of today's health-related marketing claims, convincing consumers to buy foods using promises that they would improve one's physical well-being. They also pioneered an approach to marketing that eventually influenced virtually every sector of the economy: creating a need where one hadn't previously existed and then offering a product to fill it.

Because Postum, a hot beverage, was popular during winter months, Post designed a complimentary product that could be eaten cold to increase his sales during warmer weather. He introduced his Grape Nuts cereal, consisting of nuggets of maltose and wheat. It made use of the parts of the wheat which remained after the bran had been removed to make Postum, enabling Post to cut down on waste while bringing a new item to market. Not surprisingly, considering Post's advertising history, Grape Nuts contained neither grapes nor nuts. The proprietor budgeted heavily for his marketing endeavors, told the public that the product rendered appendectomies unnecessary, and launched the first wildly successful breakfast cereal. The popularity of Grape Nuts drew an onslaught of entrepreneurs to Battle Creek, all of them determined to make their fortunes producing and distributing healthy foods. Visitors who came to town to be treated at the San were greeted by hawkers trying to sell them shares of these budding enterprises.

The world of American food would never be the same. Out of the larger-than-life landscape and the abundance that it offered, the country's entrepreneurs had managed to create an antidote that was as sensational as the poison. The Battle Creek cereal manufacturers stepped in to help heal the pathologies created by a diet built on phenomenal excess, but they did so in a phenomenally excessive way, with exaggerated health claims and unprecedented marketing campaigns. It is no accident that these products, which grew out of a sincere movement to popularize a better way to eat, eventually came to be so loaded with sugar that they are now more a part of the problem than a step towards a solution.

Scientific Marvels

HE FATHER OF modern chemistry was a nineteenth-century Prussian named Justus von Liebig, son of a practical chemist who manufactured paint and boot polish. Leibig spent his career torn between abstract principles and practical applications, prematurely marketing flawed products based on theoretical discoveries. His most famous venture was Liebig's Extract of Meat, a condensed food still sold today under the auspices of the international conglomerate Unilever. Liebig's extract was the predecessor of modern powdered soups and bouillon cubes. During his day, the product came under fire from fellow chemists and businessmen debating whether the most healthful concentrate could be produced by boiling meat quickly or simmering it at low temperatures. The actual answer to this question was ultimately less important than the technique of reducing whole, fresh food to a portable, shelf-stable product.

Liebig was a devoted student of the fundamental building blocks of soil and food. He unraveled the chemical composition of arable earth and found that its basic components were carbon, hydrogen, oxygen, nitrogen, and phosphorous. The first three elements are readily available in air and water. Liebig believed that nitrogen, like carbon, hydrogen, and oxygen, could be easily restored to the soil once it was depleted because it is present in such substantial quantities in the atmosphere. He was wrong: the nitrogen in the air is tightly bonded, or nonreactive. In fact, until the twentieth century, the only way to access the nitrogen necessary to grow healthy plants was to cultivate leguminous species such as beans and clover, which have the unique quality of being "nitrogen fixing," or bonding with the nitrogen in the air and making it available to the soil.

The age-old technique of crop rotation generally included periodic planting of a leguminous cover crop, which would be plowed under to boost fertility. Liebig hoped that his new molecular understanding of soil's chemistry could replace this longstanding practice—which required taking tracts of land out of production every second or third year—with a new strategy of directly replacing the necessary elements. In theory, this would have dramatically increased yields, allowing more land to be planted during a greater share of the available time. In practice, Liebig's incomplete understanding of healthy soil rendered this profound insight mostly useless, at least until 1909 when a German Jewish scientist named Fritz Haber discovered a technique for directly extracting nitrogen from the air.

Liebig himself was primarily interested in developing an agricultural product based on the element phosphorous by developing and marketing a commercial fertilizer intended to restore the element to the soil. He worked closely with English scientists after a trip to the British Isles showed him the profound suffering of the Irish people during the potato famine. Although this tragedy was caused by a pathogen rather than a shortage of nutrients in the soil, it was a glaring example of the failure of contemporary agriculture to adequately feed a hungry population.

The prevailing wisdom of the time espoused the "humus theory," or the idea that soil was nourished and regenerated by decaying organic matter. Liebig instead stressed the important role that chemical elements played in building healthy soil. Ironically, after twentieth-century industrial agriculture took Liebig's insight to an extreme, relying unduly on chemical fertilizers and causing widespread ecological damage, contemporary organic farmers have returned to a modern version of the humus theory, making composting into an art and a science. The pitfall of Liebig's approach to studying the nature of soil was an incomplete understanding of its enormous complexity and of the importance of micronutrients and microorganisms. Even today, we don't fully comprehend the organic and chemical processes taking place in the ground where we grow our food.

In addition to this unwarranted certainty about soil's chemical composition, Liebig's fertilizer products were prone to technical difficulty. Working with English partners in manufacturing and business, Liebig designed six chemical mixes targeted towards farmers growing a variety of crops. The ingredients were fused in a furnace to produce clumps that would break down over time, rather than melting into the soil all at once. But the entrepreneurs never tested the fertilizer. The chunks did not break down easily when the fields were watered, but rather lay uselessly on top. An extra round of plowing would have solved the problem, but the product was designed to make farming easier, rather than adding extra steps. Farmers stopped using it, and Liebig's ideas lost credibility in Britain.

In the end, Liebig's specific conclusions about what it would take to nourish the soil and properly feed the human body were less important than his broader insight that organic matter is made up of inorganic components. In theory, an understanding of the chemical composition of living things could improve our diets and enable us to grow food more efficiently. In practice, the implementation of incomplete knowledge about profoundly complex processes yielded results that were inferior to empirical folk wisdom developed over the course of millennia about how to eat and farm. Liebig's rush-to-market products based on superficial conclusions yielded products with dubious practical value. Since his day, the application of chemistry to food production has enabled manufacturers to add vital nutrients to their products; it has also given them the technology to produce shelf-stable foods that, more often than not, are nutritionally inadequate.

Over in France, a fellow chemist named Louis Pasteur was also exploring the relationship between organic and inorganic matter, drawing theoretical conclusions with far-reaching practical results. There was long distance acrimony between the two men—not least because their countries were involved in longstanding disputes over territory—but they managed to extend the discord to the field of science, as well. Liebig, who was twenty years Pasteur's senior, openly criticized some of his younger colleague's early achievements, most notably his discovery of the fact that fermentation is a biological rather than a chemical process. History has proven Pasteur to be the winner in this dispute, but to a young chemist painstakingly building a reputation, this stinging criticism from a leader in his field was deeply painful.

The emperor Napoleon III personally commissioned Pasteur to study fermentation to help save the French wine industry. As a result of changes in the system of land ownership in France following the revolution, many small-scale farmers were able to become independent operators, tending vineyards. But the wines of these inexperienced vintners turned to vinegar too quickly and were also prone to mold. Pasteur analyzed samples of spoiled and unspoiled wines under the microscope, learning to recognize beneficial and harmful microorganisms. He supplemented his laboratory studies with empirical observations, smelling and tasting the different wines, searching for patterns that matched sensory data with lab results.

Pasteur's contemporaries fiercely debated whether the newly discovered microorganisms could spring into life spontaneously or whether they came from some source invisible to the naked eye. Pasteur was firmly against the theory of spontaneous generation, maintaining that tiny organisms could be found almost everywhere, and failure to detect them was due to faulty experimental techniques. He went so far as to collect air samples from very high altitudes, proving that tiny forms of life were present even in atmosphere that was rarefied and pure.

His passionate resistance to the idea of spontaneous generation spurred Pasteur to search for conditions that promoted the growth of microorganisms. By asking the right questions, he identified the reason that so much of his country's wine was spoiling prematurely: the wrong microorganisms were replicating too quickly. To remedy the situation, he devised the technique known today as "pasteurization." We most commonly associate this process with milk and dairy products, but it first came into widespread usage among vintners. Pasteur built on the work of another Frenchman named Nicholas Appert, who had discovered earlier in the century that heating foods to high temperatures made them shelf stable. Appert fathered the technology of canning. He observed empirically that this method was effective, though nobody knew why it worked until Pasteur's work with microorganisms provided the final puzzle piece.

The technique of pasteurization proved to be controversial, even in Pasteur's day. Winemakers insisted that heating wine destroyed its flavor. True to form, Pasteur assembled a panel of experts to blind taste and compare pasteurized and unpasteurized wine. They concluded that the pasteurized wines tasted no different from those that had not undergone the process. Nonetheless, the debate over pasteurization and flavor continues even today, as aficionados of raw milk cheeses argue that the pasteurization process ruins the complex taste of their product.

After he proved himself indispensable to the wine growers, France's agricultural minister asked Pasteur to work with the country's livestock farmers to eradicate anthrax. Once again, his keen powers of observation and rigorous experimental methodology led him to insights which had eluded earlier scientists. After identifying the microorganism that apparently caused the disease, he sought to understand its spread by examining the conditions where it proliferated. He observed that sheep in his laboratory, fed alfalfa drenched in a broth containing the cultured microbe, were less likely to contract the disease than sheep that grazed in fields where the pathogen was present. He deduced that grass and hay spread the disease: being sharper than the soft alfalfa in the lab, they caused microscopic cuts that allowed the bacteria to infiltrate the animals' systems.

By drawing these conclusions, Pasteur helped to rejuvenate France's meat and dairy industries. His insight about the role of microscopic pathogens in plant, animal, and human ailments ultimately changed the science of food processing. The fact that we wash our hands before handling food is a direct consequence of Pasteur's work, as are the protocols that food safety inspectors use today when tracking food-borne illness.

The widespread use of chemical preservatives also has roots in Pasteur's work. He repeatedly observed that substances such as boric and carbolic acids inhibited the growth of bacteria. Although he did not apply this insight to food preservation per se, food processors began experimenting with chemicals such as sodium benzoate which could extend the shelf lives of their products. Technologies for pickling and salting food existed thousands of years before anyone observed the presence of microorganisms under a microscope, but this new understanding of food chemistry and biology opened the door for countless new applications of preservation techniques. This was a mixed blessing: on the one hand, making perishable food last longer feeds hungry populations year round; on the other hand, many of the substances used to commercially preserve food over the years have proven to be toxic.

American industry, in particular, embraced the use of chemical preservatives, so much so that by 1879 European countries began restricting the sale of American food products. In response, federal legislators tried to pass laws restricting the use of harmful additives, but the idea did not have widespread support. Individual states implemented their own guidelines, creating a confusing patchwork of legislation. Catsup products, in particular, were heavily adulterated with chemicals to preserve shelf life, and with artificial coloring to disguise the unsavory hue that characterized many brands in their original states. The tomato-based condiment was one of the most commonly produced items during the early days of industrial food manufacturing with hundreds of brands available in the United States. The basic recipe could easily be made into a relatively shelf-stable product—with the help of preservatives—and it was a convenient way for producers to use bruised tomatoes, as well as peels and cores which were trimmed before the tomatoes made their way to the cannery.

A researcher named Harvey Wiley, chief chemist at the USDA at the turn of the century, took a strong stance against the use of artificial colorings and chemical preservatives. He found support from a handful of manufacturers who were concerned about the European bans on their products. These forward-thinking entrepreneurs saw the potential benefit of having an ally in the form of a public servant who could help them devise alternative technologies. Most producers began steering away from some of the more dangerous preservatives such as salicylic and boric acids, but they were convinced that their products couldn't survive without some chemical help, and they believed sodium benzoate to be the least toxic option. Wiley did experiments feeding the chemical to volunteers, most of whom became dangerously ill. But the manufacturers claimed that they could use little enough of the substance in their products to render them benign.

Wiley diligently tested product samples to determine whether they contained harmful chemicals, and he also investigated the effects of these additives on humans. At the same time, he supervised research designed to find other ways to keep food from spoiling. He found that the use of scraps rejected during the process of canning tomatoes—the very practice that made ketchup such an appealing choice for producers—caused product to turn putrid. These bruised trimmings were rife with the microorganisms that caused fermentation and spoilage. Wiley and his associates experimented with producing ketchup from fresh, clean tomatoes and adjusting the quantities of sugar, salt, and vinegar, which also increased shelf life.

Eventually, some manufacturers began changing their practices and eschewing the use of preservatives and artificial colorings. The Heinz Company was the largest and most visible establishment to do so, taking the opportunity to turn their new practices into a highly successful marketing campaign. They let everyone know that their ketchup was superior because they used high-quality ingredients and manufactured it in an immaculate facility. They were the forerunners of many of today's organic and natural food companies, who use old fashioned, common-sense strategies to produce clean products, using purity and common sense as selling points.

This controversy took place in the context of a growing public awareness about the horrifying practices taking place in some Chicago slaughterhouses that came to light with the publication of Upton Sinclair's muckraking novel, *The Jungle*, which appeared in serial form in 1905. The book described foul-smelling packing rooms, rotten meat, and dead rodents mixed in with sausage filling. Though Sinclair had originally intended the work to generate outrage about labor conditions rather than unsanitary practices in the plants, the outcry generated by his descriptions finally motivated legislators to pass bills mandating standards for the purity and cleanliness of food products. The Pure Food and Drugs Act and the Meat Inspection Act of 1906 were aimed at implementing measures to control the quality of the country's food supply by keeping it free from food-borne illnesses and harmful chemical additives. Producers were now required by law to honestly label their products so consumers would know what was actually in them.

Although the legislation was ostensibly intended to protect consumers from dangerous manufacturing practices, large-scale food producers—especially the meatpacking companies—played an important role in crafting the law. It had become plain to them that they needed to at least create the illusion that they were working to protect their customers from the potential dangers that lurked in the food they ate. While consumers certainly benefitted from having some oversight in place, the legislation was largely a missed opportunity to take some real steps to ensure the production of safer food, especially meat. Enforcement of its provisions was left largely up to the Department of Agriculture, an agency geared towards protecting the business interests of the very producers it was supposed to be policing. Rather than making it the responsibility of the meat packers to guarantee a safe product, the law relied on government safety inspectors to spot problems. In addition, federal inspection was only required for products crossing state lines. This actually provided a marketing advantage to large meat conglomerates, which were now able to show a seal of credibility not available to their smaller competitors.

DURING THE LATE eighteenth and early nineteenth centuries, chemists began isolating and identifying the major building blocks of food: fats, proteins, and carbohydrates. Since that time, scientists studying nutrition have argued for the relative importance of one of these elements—usually protein—over the others. Liebig compared protein with nitrogen, the central component in soil; the food pyramid designed by the USDA during the 1990s placed carbohydrates at the foundation of the structure. Today most sensible nutritionists concur that all three macronutrients are essential for good health; they also generally agree that we need a wide range of additional substances in smaller amounts.

Although the word "vitamin" wasn't coined until 1912, eighteenth-century seamen discovered that vitamin C was indispensable for good health when they found that fresh fruits and vegetables prevented the life-threatening disease scurvy during long sea voyages. A hundred years later researchers studying the condition beriberi in Indonesia concluded that the culprit was white or "polished" rice, which lacked nutrients provided by the whole grain. These discoveries paralleled others suggesting traditional methods of preparing foods created more healthful alternatives than emerging modern food-processing techniques. Nineteenth-century innovations enabled millers to grind wheat and corn between metal rollers, rather than primitive grinding stones, cheaply producing the kinds of highly refined flours that had previously been available only to the wealthy. The urban poor of Europe, who subsisted mainly on bread, lost access to the B vitamins in the wheat germ that was now sifted out of their flour.

Similarly, when food processors began grinding corn with metal rollers, they produced flour that lacked the important trace minerals which had flaked off of traditional grinding stones. These tiny chips added essential alkaline nutrients to the corn, making it substantially more nourishing and digestible than in its original state. The act of processing corn with alkaline ingredients such as ash and lime is known as "nixtmalization." It had been practiced since ancient times, especially among Central American tribes who relied heavily on corn for sustenance. When corn became a subsistence food in Italy during the eighteenth and nineteenth centuries, the nutritional deficiency disease pellagra became widespread, although Native Americans hadn't typically suffered from the ailment. Researchers studying the problem eventually discovered that the modern European milling techniques created a product that lacked niacin and other essential B vitamins.

During the early years of the twentieth century, an American dentist named Weston Price grew alarmed at the state of many of the teeth he was examining and began wondering whether there was a link between diet and dental health. To investigate the matter, he traveled extensively, studying the teeth and diets of indigenous populations. He visited communities in isolated parts of Europe, the Arctic, Africa, Southeast Asia, Melanesia, and South America. In each case, he looked for groups who were similar genetically, some of whom had adopted a typical Western diet, and some of whom continued to eat traditional foods. He even studied siblings in families that had made the conversion from indigenous to modern foods before younger brothers or sisters were born. It is fortunate that Price performed his research when he did because it would have been nearly impossible today: there simply aren't enough communities remaining that are entirely unaffected by the spread of modern foods.

Price's results were clear and profound. In almost every case, people who had continued to eat the foods that their ancestors had eaten had strong, straight, healthy teeth. He also found correlations between diets of processed foods and incidence of tuberculosis, goiter, and orthopedic difficulties. He used a rigorous scientific approach, looking for control groups and calculating the percentage of dental caries in each community relative to the total number of teeth he examined and also relative to the number of individuals. He took exhaustive photographs of indigenous people with both healthy and unhealthy teeth. Despite his precise methodology, there is a deeply human aspect to his work. Most of his photographs show people proudly displaying their teeth, a demeanor which reflected genuine trust and rapport between the researcher and his subjects. Their willingness—even eagerness—to participate in his studies is understandable. As Price related, many of them fully understood that they lived better and felt healthier when they ate the foods that their ancestors had enjoyed.

Weston repeatedly referred to the high moral character of the people he met who based their diets on traditional foods. Cowherds in Switzerland's high-altitude Loetschantal Valley had no need to lock their doors because nobody would think of stealing anything there. He described the dispositions of rats in experimental situations: those fed exclusively on white flour were aggressive and irritable while those that ate bran and other nutrients generally absent from processed foods were healthy and sweet tempered. These observations lack the scientific rigor of his statistical analyses of dental caries, but they prefigure some of the work being done today as we learn that students with learning and behavioral disorders perform better in school when they are weaned off of junk food, and prison populations show signs of rehabilitation when they maintain organic gardens and eat fresh vegetables.

Weston analyzed the traditional staples of the healthy indigenous populations he studied. Like many people consuming Western diets, these populations subsisted on a narrow range of foods. But the quality of their provisions was far superior to those available in industrialized societies. Weston paid special attention to the nutritional content of butter, discovering that when it is made from milk from cows eating grass in the most prolific phase of its growth cycle—usually in early spring—it contained unusually high amounts of vitamin A.

In alpine Swiss villages where Weston studied healthy subjects with traditional diets, herds grazed on mountains covered with snow for much of the year. Higher-altitude pastures became available over the course of the spring and summer as the ice pack melted. The animals ate grass right near the snow line; as the season progressed, snow at higher altitudes melted, and new grass was exposed. In this manner, the cows were able to consume grass at the most nutritious phase of its life cycle for an extended period of time. The rye bread that these Swiss villagers ate with their cheese was also more nutritious than the loaves consumed in the industrialized world, in part because of unrefined flour and also because the grain was grown in soil that was regularly fertilized with manure and not depleted by over-production. Again, Weston anticipated nutritional insights that we are only now beginning to understand as organic farmers develop a range of strategies for returning nutrients to their fields and consumers grasp the fact that better food grows in better soil.

In the Outer Hebrides islands off the coast of northwest Scotland, Weston found healthy people living on a diet of small fish and oat cakes. Among Inuit tribes in northern Canada, he encountered communities eating primarily salmon, seal oil, and fish eggs. Native American tribes in the Yukon Territory and British Columbia enjoyed the bear and moose that they hunted and had detailed knowledge of the healing power of specific animals' internal organs. Melanesians in the South Pacific hunted for wild pigs in the bush and fished for tremendous coconut crabs in the sea. The Masai of Africa lived on the meat, milk, and blood of their cattle, and Peruvian Indians along the Amazon basin feasted on tropical fruits and vegetables as well as abundant fish from the river.

Why did people all over the world stop eating time-tested diets that clearly nourished them better than modern alternatives? In many cases, colonization robbed them of the resources they needed to continue consuming traditional diets. Hunting and gathering require wide open landscapes, which were no longer available once settlers began claiming plots and using them for farming and industry. Surely it seemed easier to open a package of something sweet or starchy than to comb through the bush for prey or scour the waters for fish. These unfamiliar foods must also have held a genuine allure, at least initially, especially for the younger generations. We see a similar phenomenon today as American fast-food restaurants export their chains around the globe. Teenagers embrace the easy availability of french fries and hamburgers to the dismay of their parents and grandparents. For the indigenous peoples Weston studied, the adverse health effects of their new diets were not apparent at first but became all too obvious over time.

In industrialized nations, the emerging knowledge that processed foods did not provide adequate nutrition opened the door for powerful new marketing strategies as manufacturers learned to use Liebig's approach of distilling vital elements and compounds and then adding them back into processed foods. As the cereal moguls of the nineteenth century proved, people are eager to buy foods that they believe will make them healthier. The aisles of today's supermarkets are piled high with products whose labels boast of healthful additives, from oat bran to omega-3 fatty acids. On some level, these fortified foods reflect contemporary research regarding specific elements that have the capacity to fight disease and keep our bodies operating well. But we wouldn't have to reconstruct the nutritional value of good, simple food if we hadn't lost our connection to it in the first place.

The Inconvenience of Convenience

MODERN PROCESSED FOOD came of age with the Industrial Revolution. As rural families traded their chickens, kitchen gardens, and stew pots for cramped, urban rooms, they came to rely on convenience food products and street vendors for daily sustenance. Some consumers must have found this change liberating, particularly displaced farmers' wives who had traditionally been occupied during virtually all of their waking hours maintaining households, preparing meals, and processing raw materials into usable staples. Work in the early factory towns also involved long and grueling days, but when laborers left the factory at the end of a shift, their jobs were done. There were even occasional days with no work at all, unlike farm life, where cows needed to be milked even on the Sabbath.

The transition from a largely self-sufficient rural existence to a modern urban lifestyle did not take place all at once. D.H. Lawrence's *Sons and Lovers*, first published in 1913, described the life of a collier's family living in a mining town. They baked their own bread, kept a kitchen garden, foraged for wild plants, and dried herbs for tea and medicine. No doubt they did so in part for financial reasons, but they also took pride in these tasks and ate a better diet than they would have if they subsisted merely on the processed foods available in the company store. Their knowledge of how to draw sustenance out of the landscape was both a practical resource and a source of identity and pride, drawing on the knowledge and experience of many generations.

Like the first Neolithic farmers transitioning from hunting and gathering to working the land, early industrial workers must have felt both relief and wistfulness about switching to a new way of eating and living. Unlike the Neolithic revolution, the Industrial Revolution is still recent enough for us to have first-hand accounts in art, literature, and folklore. The ideology of Marxism and the poetry of the Romantic period can be read as reactions to industrial modernization. Karl Marx envisioned an economic system founded on honest work, rather than accumulated capital, as an alternative to the dehumanizing conditions he witnessed in Europe's factories. The Romantic poets yearned for a pastoral landscape, a return to peaceful, agrarian ways.

As technologies improved, store-bought food products became more diverse and interesting, and marketing strategies grew more sophisticated. One of the earliest mass-produced foods was the biscuit, or what we think of today as a cracker. These hard, durable staples had been produced for centuries to feed navies and seamen on long voyages. In London during the early nineteenth century, a Quaker named Jonathan Dickson Carr invented the mechanical biscuit stamp, which streamlined production. George Palmer, another of his countrymen, devised a process for rolling the biscuits both backwards and forwards, doubling efficiency. Palmer became partners with another established biscuit maker, Joseph Huntley, whose son manufactured metal tins for his product. This packaging was an ingenious marketing gimmick. Customers reused the tins, keeping the company's name and logo in plain view. Explorers even found the containers on remote islands where few other trappings of Western civilization had yet arrived.

In the United States during the nineteenth century, biscuits had typically been sold in "cracker barrels," or containers at the general store that were stocked by wholesalers, pouring new product on top of the old, letting the crumbs and pieces fall to the bottom of the heap. During the later part of the century, Nabisco and the National Biscuit Company took advantage of the growing fear of germs to wrap their products in sanitary-looking packages. The National Biscuit Company named their product "Uneeda Biscuit," a pun novel enough to be successful. The strategy of packaging products with an emphasis on cleanliness and purity came about in response to consumer demand, and the companies' advertising reinforced the perception that the traditional way of selling biscuits was unsanitary and unsafe.

Canned foods provide another example of the symbiotic relationship between the emerging industrial working class and the manufacturers who employed them and also sold them products tailored to their new circumstances. Like the popular biscuits, canned foods were originally produced for military purposes, to provision forces during extended excursions. During the Napoleonic campaigns, the French chemist Nicholas Appert developed the technique of heating food in a sealed container in order to render it shelf stable. Manufacturers began preserving meat and vegetables in glass jars, and then they started using tin cans as well. The process of fabricating the earliest metal cans was labor-intensive, and they were not widely used until the middle of the nineteenth century when engineers devised a process for mechanically attaching and sealing the lids.

This new development increased the efficiency of the canning process twentyfold. Tinned food products were largely responsible for feeding soldiers on both sides of the conflict in the American Civil War. Arctic explorers brought them on their frigid journeys; in fact, botulism resulting from improper canning techniques probably killed the crew of Sir John Franklin's famous expedition in search of the Northwest Passage.

When the technology was in its infancy, canned foods were prohibitively expensive and therefore available mainly to wealthy consumers. Their high price and the novelty of being able to eat fruits and vegetables out of season lent them allure in spite of the fact that preserved foods generally do not taste as good as fresh ones and are nutritionally inferior. As manufacturing processes grew more sophisticated and prices dropped, canned foods came into everyday usage for working-class families, especially those who lacked the time and cooking equipment to prepare fresh meals from scratch. This development not only satisfied consumers who needed convenient food products, it also benefited entrepreneurs who were eager to embrace any new application of the profitable, industrial model of mass production.

Over time, storefronts selling a range of packaged, manufactured foods began to replace the traditional marketplace, where small-scale specialized vendors operated stalls and sold homemade items directly to consumers. During the early industrial era, both types of sales venues operated simultaneously, but grocers mainly stocked imported items such as tea, spices, and sugar and sold them by weight rather than in labeled packages. As producers began developing techniques for creating foods that could last longer, these grocers began carrying a wider range of packaged products, eventually supplanting the public marketplace as a source of everyday staples.

This development was convenient for consumers because they didn't have to shop as often or haggle with as many proprietors, and it opened new possibilities for entrepreneurs to develop a range of offerings and promote them in novel ways. The modern advertising industry was born with this shift in the way that urban dwellers shopped for food. Instead of relying on face-to-face contact with the folks who grew their vegetables and raised the animals that went into their meat products, potential buyers now needed new ways to obtain information about the foods they bought. Creative businessmen like C.W. Post ran newspaper and magazine ads, hung signs in public places, and distributed free samples and knickknacks at public events, as the Heinz Company did so successfully at the Chicago World's Fair in 1892, when they gave out tens of thousands of pickle pins. Entrepreneurs used creative strategies for branding, packaging, and naming their products to encourage potential shoppers to choose them from among the many offerings on the shelves of neighborhood grocery stores.

The gulf between producers and consumers widened as manufacturers discovered the enormous power of advertising to introduce their products to customers far from the factories that made them. The adulteration of foods with artificial fillers, preservatives, and colorings became commonplace, generating a need for legislation to ensure that manufacturers told the truth about what they put in their cans and bottles. This type of dishonesty certainly had a very long history, from the town millers who laced their flour with sand and sawdust to increase its weight to the local brewers who watered down their ale. But it became increasingly problematic as consumers lost the firsthand contact they'd traditionally had with food merchants. If the miller down the road cheated you, you could confront him face-to-face. But if a company on the other side of the country produced a tainted product that made you sick, it was harder to hold it accountable.

The revolution in food production and packaging coincided with changes in cooking techniques and equipment. Traditionally, most families had cooked over a hearth or fireplace, hanging pots over the fire and baking bread and cakes in spots that weren't in direct contact with the flame. During the mid-nineteenth century manufacturers began producing stoves for home use with separate chambers for ovens as well as stovetop burners with adjustable flames. These new appliances were marketed for the convenience they offered as well as the superior meals that homemakers could create with them.

Unlike a can of fish or beans from the neighborhood store, the purchase of a stove was a considerable investment. The kitchens of the wealthy had been filled with such equipment for centuries with flocks of servants fussing over the household's daily needs. New manufacturing technologies now made these appliances available to the middle class as well. They were especially popular in kitchens on American homesteads, where farmwives made meals from scratch for ravenous work crews.

In the United States, new cooking methods spurred an entire field of academic research devoted to studying household labor processes to determine the most efficient ways to perform daily tasks. The field of home economics became commonplace at women's colleges, teaching everything from frugal use of ingredients to efficient strategies for operating in the kitchen. These courses aimed to free home cooks from the empirical, unscientific methods that they had previously used, enabling them to make the most of their time and resources.

Researchers in the field methodically studied every movement that was required for basic processes such as beating eggs, following home cooks with stop watches and making recommendations for more effective uses of their time and energy. These "time and motion" studies not surprisingly turned out to be deeply flawed, not least because their methodologies were devised by scientists examining cooking processes outside of the complex, day-to-day context in which they commonly occurred. Like the nineteenth century scientists who tried in vain to replicate the nutritional complexity of meat and soil, they could not replace the visceral, homespun wisdom that had grown out of centuries—and even millennia—of practical, hands-on experience.

Although the ostensible objective of these studies—and the advertised purpose of the new appliances—was to simplify the work of the housewife so she could have more time for leisure activities, this rarely occurred in practice. In *The Best Thing I Ever Tasted*, Sallie Tisdale describes her mother's seemingly endless days as an ambivalent homemaker trying to feed her family and maintain her household with contemporary appliances and convenience foods. Even prepackaged mixes didn't simplify her daily tasks. Most of the canned products and seasoning packets that had come into mainstream usage in American households by the 1950s and 1960s still called for multiple steps and complex processes. Each labor saving product or device brought with it a new set of expectations and chores. Gas and electric stoves replaced fireplaces that had to be perpetually supplied with wood and kindling, but in the process, home cooks lost the ease of the stew pot that simmered all day, making meals out of scraps. Over time, the stove was joined by the toaster oven, mix master, juicer, and coffee grinder, all gadgets that created new expectations and required additional cleaning.

As soup and cake mixes came to be replaced by TV dinners and microwaves, the work of the homemaker did get easier, but this ease came with a cost. The idea of a prepackaged meal that could be reheated with a minimum of effort and eaten by a solitary individual in front of a television set replaced traditional mealtime conviviality. Ironically, TV dinners were first marketed as conducive to family values. A 1954 ad for Swanson's shows a proud father in a frilly apron bearing two steaming trays for his children. "Now Dad's an expert at 'frying up' a chicken dinner!"

The father of the TV dinner was an entrepreneur named Jeffrey Schaffer who devised the product as a way to make use of 520,000 pounds of surplus turkey, along with an extra batch of metal tins. As he experimented with the product, he devised the tray compartments that separated the different "courses," an innovation that played a vital role in the format's popularity by keeping the individual components from getting soggy. But the TV dinner was more than just a lucky design inspired by leftover materials. Like the canned foods of the Industrial Age and the appliances of the twentieth century, the frozen dinner filled a niche for producers and consumers alike.

Manufacturers had found a "value added" product in the richest sense. The cost of the ingredients that went into these dinners was minimal and growing lower all the time as new fertilizing methods improved agricultural efficiency and factory feedlots streamlined and cheapened food production. The design, packaging, and novelty of the product allowed companies to charge high prices, at least initially. The first TV dinners cost 98 cents, the price of seven loaves of bread. By advertising the ease of preparation, producers were able to tap into the insatiable demand for convenience that had been generated by the routines of the modern workplace and also by their own relentless marketing machine.

The very form of entertainment which gave its name to the TV dinner played a fundamental role in changing modern consumption habits. It offered role models, examples of how "normal" families behaved and spent their time. It also provided a powerful advertising venue that stimulated multiple senses simultaneously. The emphasis on individual taste rhapsodized by early French gastronomists found powerful new expression with this current wave of consumerism. Each family member could eat a different meal if they chose to do so, one that suited his personal preference.

In addition to the TV dinner, the 1950s saw the emergence of another convenience food trend that would eventually change eating habits all over the world. Fast-food restaurants came of age during the post-war era in the United States, filling a niche that had been created by widespread car ownership and large-scale paving of roads, as well as the consequent migrations from urban areas to suburbs. All of these developments came about in part because of the broad-based affluence during that period, and they acted in tandem to generate new consumer needs that could be filled with products easily purchased with disposable income.

There was nothing especially new about the idea of offering convenient food in locations primarily patronized by customers who arrived by car. Drive-ins and burger joints had been growing in popularity since the 1930s, especially in Southern California, the quintessential suburban landscape. But a new era began in the late forties, when two brothers named Richard and Maurice McDonald began rethinking the systems at their Burger Bar with an eye towards consistency and efficiency. They streamlined their menu, lowered their prices, and retooled their operation so their kitchen functioned in much the same way as Henry

Ford's famous auto plant, with an assembly line that dramatically increased production speed. They divided their processes into discrete, repetitive tasks that could be performed by workers without any special skills or training. Customers placed their orders at the counter rather than waiting for tableside service.

The brothers' place was popular, especially among families who couldn't afford to eat out in more expensive restaurants, and it spawned many imitators. But its crowning moment came in 1954 when a milkshake machine salesman named Ray Kroc convinced the McDonalds to let him franchise their concept nationwide. For Kroc, the operation itself was a product that could be marketed and sold to aspiring proprietors looking for a relatively foolproof venture. Because the operation was so profitable and efficient, it provided a far less risky investment for a franchisee than the ordeal of starting a business independently from scratch. Kroc set about branding the restaurant and its products through television and billboards, making it the most widely recognized name in America and, eventually, the world. As he and his staff began to grasp the power of advertising directly to children, they devised campaigns and specifically targeted the next generation of consumers. The Ronald McDonald icon, the bright, convenient playgrounds, the free toys, and the cross-marketing with popular children's movies all proved to be wildly successful strategies for luring children and insuring that they'd convince their parents to buy them Big Macs and Happy Meals.

The success of these marketing efforts was instrumental in changing the landscape of food production. Never before had a single operation controlled such a large share of the food supply. McDonald's itself used a staggering quantity of raw materials, and its success spawned a host of other chain restaurants, from Burger King to Pizza Hut to Taco Bell. Together they created an aggregate demand that made use of the economies of scale that had been evolving since the beginning of the Industrial Revolution, taking them to unprecedented levels. Flavors were artificially synthesized by laboratory technicians using chemicals to replicate genuine taste sensations. Slaughterhouses became considerably more gruesome and dangerous than they had been during Upton Sinclair's day. Potatoes were bred to yield an optimum number of french fries.

Advertisements for fast-food restaurants naturally emphasized the supposed benefits for the consumer. McDonald's "Have it Your Way" commercials touted their willingness to personalize their offerings, in the spirit of centuries of enterprising entrepreneurs. More recently, their "I'm Loving It" campaign made an explicit connection between eating fast-food products and living well. But ultimately, the advantages reaped from the fast-food industry have accrued to proprietors at the expense of their workers and customers. These operations pay the lowest possible wages, consistently lobbying against laws mandating higher pay. Despite the fact that everything from cashier greetings to the size of french fries is standardized at McDonald's locations, franchisees are free to determine how much they will pay their employees. This policy insulates corporate headquarters from charges of institutionalizing the practice of offering low wages. Fast-food restaurant managers consistently disregard employees' personal needs, scheduling workers and then sending them home if business is slow. They assign employees shifts that change from week to week, making it difficult for them to plan or find supplementary jobs. These practices extract profit at the expense of workers' personal lives, contributing to the short-term nature of much fast-food employment.

The brief tenure of most employees also works in the interests of the industry: short-term employees command low wages and receive no benefits. The industry's high rate of turnover makes it virtually impossible for workers to establish unions. Staffs at various McDonald's have taken steps towards organizing, but these efforts take time, and many employees leave before they come to fruition. The company puts considerable effort into blocking unionization, sending experienced managers to investigate when they learn that workers at a particular location have expressed an interest in organizing. Only one North American McDonald's has ever succeeded in unionizing. This location, near Montreal, was shut down soon after workers set the union certification process in motion.

The very nature of the work—compartmentalized and repetitive—ensures that there is little opportunity for workers to advance and earn more money. This is not to say that fast-food work is easy or requires little skill. The relentless pace, hot and dangerous conditions, and need for impeccable timing make these jobs demanding. The increasing mechanization of the industry neither simplifies tasks nor eliminates positions. Rather, technology enables workers to produce more product in less time under considerable pressure.

The fast-food industry's lack of regard for the dignity and safety of its workers extends from restaurant staff to the employees of its suppliers. Slaughterhouse workers endure especially hazardous conditions. Their rate of serious injury is higher than that of any other segment of the economy. Because cows, unlike chickens, vary considerably in size and shape, they need to be processed manually with sharp knives. The tools used by the beef-packing industry have not changed much since the turn of the century, but the speed of the line has increased more than tenfold. This fast-paced work with sharp implements creates an especially treacherous work environment.

The fast-food industry has taken its toll on its regular customers as well. The American epidemics of obesity, diabetes, and heart disease cannot be blamed exclusively on the cheap, quick, convenient food available at these outlets, but the frequency of consumption along with the inferior quality of the food has certainly correlated with an increase in diet-related ailments. In 2004, obesity replaced smoking as the leading cause of preventable death in the United States. Child-based advertising campaigns successfully lure customers at a particularly vulnerable age, when the marketing gimmicks, the food's homogeneity, and the soft drinks' sweetness ensure a fierce brand loyalty that persists into teenage and adult years. Franchises in high school and college cafeterias, as well as a landscape covered with accessible locations, make fast food a daily meal choice for many Americans, and increasingly for consumers all over the world.

The trend towards obesity parallels an increase in portion sizes at restaurants, and even among home cooks. A recent study comparing the recipes in the contemporary edition of the *Joy of Cooking* with the first edition, which was first published seventy-three years earlier, found that on average the recipes in the new version contained nearly fifty percent more calories than the ones in the original book. The researchers attributed the change to the fact that today's dishes call for a greater number of high-calorie ingredients and also noted that the serving sizes themselves were smaller in the earlier version. They conjectured that the recipes included more rich foods because the relative prices of these items had declined during the intervening seventy-three years.

This change in the affordability of high-calorie foods such as meat, cheese, and processed sweeteners has come about largely because of technological developments that enable us to produce larger quantities of low-quality food. Factory farms raise animals in cramped conditions, feeding them antibiotics and growth hormones to make them gain weight quickly, and then shipping them to the killing floor without taking the time to determine whether they are healthy or ill. Industrial farming operations use petrochemicals to artificially increase yields, depleting the soil and growing crops with inferior nutritional value.

Government programs encourage overproduction, with subsidies aimed at keeping prices low. The prevailing approach of the American government towards agriculture during the past thirty years has been to give farmers financial incentives to plant "from fencerow to fencerow," in the words of Earl Butz, who held the position of Secretary of Agriculture during the 1970s, when high meat prices spurred angry housewives to boycott beef and picket grocery stores. As a result of Butz's influence, the United States government began supplementing the incomes of farmers growing key crops, most notably corn and soy.

Most of this overproduction becomes feed for livestock. This practice helps to keep beef, chicken, and pork prices artificially low, but it also degrades the quality of the meat. Cattle, in particular, evolved as ruminants, eating mostly grass. The practice of feeding corn to cows didn't start with Butz's policies, but rather with many generations of farmers whose customers preferred the marbled texture of muscle meat created by a diet rich in grains. The English beef tradition, in particular, has long taken pride in producing rich, fatty cuts. Even today, artisan beef producers continually experiment to create an ideal balance between grain and grass in their livestock's diets.

But the amount of corn fed to American cows during the past thirty years has been a matter of economics, rather than artistry, and has been a major factor in the spread of new food-borne pathogens, as well as the widespread use of antibiotics to combat them. The *e coli* bug in particular has been responsible for numerous food safety scares during the past few decades and can be directly traced to livestock feeding protocols. The practice of feeding livestock more corn than their systems can handle creates an unnaturally acidic condition in the ruminants' stomachs. During the past thirty years, an especially lethal strain of *e coli* has evolved, one which thrives in this acidic environment. It has caused illnesses and death not just among people who consume affected cattle but also in people who eat vegetables that have been contaminated by runoff from nearby grazing areas.

The overproduction of corn has also spurred food scientists to devise new products from the crop, which has proven to be extraordinarily versatile, yielding everything from plastics to sweeteners. As a result, high fructose corn syrup has replaced cane and beet sugar in most commercial soft drinks, making them sweeter and cheaper to produce. The corn syrup lobby recently launched an advertising campaign to convince television viewers that their product is no more harmful than other sugars, but there has been a strong correlation between its widespread use and rising rates of diabetes in all age groups. Even if the industry's claims are correct and our bodies process corn syrup in the same way as other sugars, the low price of corn syrup could in itself explain some of its destructiveness: if a sweetener is cheaper, then manufacturers will use more, and consumers will ingest more.

The American government's policy of mainly subsidizing a narrow range of crops has created an environment that favors large-scale enterprises, often forcing smaller operations out of business. This movement towards consolidation of land ownership in the hands of a limited number of individuals or corporations has a long history, dating back at least as far as Babylonian and Egyptian civilizations. There are examples in virtually every region in every historical period, from the feudal manors of medieval Europe to the vast nineteenth century plantations of Central and South America. Contemporary agricultural and distribution technologies have precipitated a particularly sinister manifestation of this age-old trend, enabling a limited number of players to assert a disproportionate amount of control over the way people eat all over the world.

In the United States, fifty percent of the population made a living from farming a hundred years ago, while less than two percent work the land today. Even in India, where seventy-five percent of the population still makes a living from agriculture, market forces have forced many small-scale producers to switch from a traditional subsistence approach aimed at feeding local markets to growing a limited number of crops for export. In both countries, this places independent operators in the position of competing with large-scale enterprises that can afford the technologies required to lower prices, influence consumer demand, and ultimately drive smaller competitors out of business.

These economies of scale have created profitable opportunities for fertilizer, pesticide, and seed companies as well. The modern fertilizer industry was born when a surplus of nitrogen from munitions factories was redirected towards agricultural products at the end of World War II. This development made farming considerably more productive in the short term. Plants were able to grow quickly in this chemical mix, at least initially, and agriculturalists could plant their acreage successively. This was an ostensible improvement over traditional techniques, which required farmers to let fields lie fallow in order to regenerate their vitality. But industrial agriculture has grown dependent on petrochemicals, requiring increasingly greater inputs. This approach has proven over time to be destructive to the farmland and the quality of the produce by oversimplifying the chemistry of the soil and creating food with less flavor and inferior nutritional value.

To make matters worse, nitrogen and phosphorus from these fertilizers run off into nearby rivers and streams, poisoning fish and wildlife. Rachel Carson's groundbreaking book *Silent Spring* brought this issue into the public eye in the early sixties. But pesticide use has continued during the intervening years, despite consumer demand for organic, unsprayed products. It has persisted in part because the companies producing these agricultural products make such a substantial profit on them. Like the insect predators which feed on fields of crops, these companies have evolved symbiotically with the industries that rely on their wares.

The practice of monoculture, or planting large, continuous areas with a single crop, makes fields especially vulnerable to insect infestations because many bugs are narrowly adapted to eat only a single variety of a single species. Traditional farming practices—and modern organic farming—control predators in part by interspersing rows of different crops so insect predators quickly run into plants that don't meet their dietary needs. This solution makes sense when produce is picked by hand, but it works against the fundamentals of mechanized, energy intensive agriculture, which relies on uniformity and consistency so that crops can be planted and harvested mechanically.

The use of pesticides continually calls for the development of newer, more powerful chemicals because genetically resistant individual insects breed succeeding generations that are not affected by the toxins. The use of these products creates a self-perpetuating cycle: farmers grow reliant on pesticides to control infestations, and they grow increasingly dependent as they encounter hardier strains that call for newly developed industrial solutions.

During the past twenty years, seed and pesticide companies have colluded—and increasingly merged—in an especially sinister approach to the issue of pest management. Scientists have learned to manipulate the genetic makeup of plants by inserting genes from other organisms with desirable qualities, such as the resistance to a particular predator or tolerance for a particular herbicide (coincidentally produced by the same company doing the research.) The resulting "genetically modified foods" have been deeply controversial; not least because the multinational companies that have invested billions of dollars developing them have put them on the market under a shroud of secrecy, fighting laws requiring them to be labeled as such.

In the United States, representatives of the biotech industry lobbied the FDA to accept their claim that genetically modified foods are essentially indistinguishable from their conventionally developed counterparts. This designation became the basis of their legal fight against identifying transgenic ingredients on food labels. But the American government's complicity has not been shared by foreign legislators. Spurred by fierce opposition from their constituents, the governments of European nations have diligently fought against pressure to import foods containing these improperly identified ingredients, spurring trade wars.

Consumer resistance to genetically modified foods comes in part from the fact that some individuals have developed severe allergies to transgenic strains, especially corn. This challenges the companies' contention that these foods are essentially identical to traditional strains that do not produce adverse reactions and indicates that, at the very least, more study and vetting is needed. In addition, there has been little oversight of the introduction of these strains into the food supply. In 2001, representatives of a consumer group tested a variety of products containing corn and found that Taco Bell taco shells contained the Star Link variety of genetically modified corn, which had been approved for use in animal feed but had shown evidence of being potentially allergenic to humans.

This news outraged even the complacent American public, and consumer groups began fighting the industry's efforts to slip these products onto the market. This reaction was in part a reaction to genuine food safety issues and practices that place corporate profits ahead of the health and well-being of their consumers, but these products also spurred a visceral fear and distaste for the arrogance of an industry that could devise a technology that toyed with new life forms in a laboratory. The term "Frankenfoods" became widely used among biotech opponents; it aptly expresses the recklessness of changing the balance of nature with insufficient concern for unintended consequences.

One such unforeseen consequence has been cross pollination between genetically modified crops and their traditionally cultivated neighbors. Although proponents of transgenic seeds insist that the potential for their crops exchanging genetic material with plants in neighboring fields in minimal, there is no question that it occurs. In one widely publicized case, the biotech giant Monsanto sued a seventy-year-old canola farmer named Percy Schmeiser from Sasketchewan, after testing a sample from his crop and finding that it contained genetic material from their patented strains. Schmeiser maintained that he had not planted the seeds himself and that they had cross-pollinated with the conventional varieties he was growing. The company initially won the case against the farmer, but he appealed and eventually prevailed. In the process, he became an international folk hero, a symbol of the worldwide resistance to the attempts of multinational corporations to appropriate the planet's seed stocks.

This issue has resonated especially strongly with the people of India who, like farmers all over the globe, have a strong tradition of saving and exchanging seeds. These seed stocks are an invaluable storehouse of genetic material, aided and preserved by the ingenuity of generations of growers who have developed crop varieties adapted to every conceivable microclimate and type of soil. These include strains that are resistant to specific pathogens and also varieties suitable for a wide range of culinary applications, with different flavors, textures, and colors. Until contemporary agricultural practice became the dominant mode of production, there were over 100,000 varieties of rice alone. Most of these subspecies were much better suited to small-scale agriculture than to industrial operations. But as agribusiness has supplanted subsistence farming in most parts of the world, planters have replaced these myriad varieties with a limited number of strains particularly suited to industrial-scale endeavors. With the advance of biotech practices, these dominant varieties have increasingly been devised in laboratories and patented so that they can be legally obtained only from the companies that developed them.

These corporations have also attempted to obtain the legal rights to names and seeds of traditional plants by using the premise that genetic material can be copyrighted. Basmati rice has been planted in India for centuries, where farmers grow twenty-seven different varieties and celebrate them in folk songs and poetry. In 1997, the Texas-based company Rice Tec tried to patent the name Basmati in order to obtain the exclusive rights to sell and market it, representing a break with the traditional rationale for issuing patents, which have historically been reserved for new innovations in order to protect the time and resources that went into developing them.

In 2001, the United States Patent and Trademark Office revoked most of the claims comprising Rice Tec's patent on basmati rice in response to a challenge from the Indian government, which was under considerable pressure from NGOs and citizens' groups. The fight to stop this type of bio-piracy is part of a worldwide grassroots movement whose mission goes far beyond protection of seed stocks. The struggle for food sovereignty represents nothing less than a fight for cultural survival, indigenous wisdom, and irreplaceable flavors.

Slowing Down

A S YOU WEAVE your way through Seattle's packed Ballard
Farmers' Market on a sunny spring Sunday, it's hard to
believe that anyone eats fast-food on a daily basis. Eager
shoppers admire ripe fruits and vegetables, lovingly choosing ingredients for their dinners. Street performers draw crowds on the
sidelines, making the food-shopping errand into its own form
of entertainment. The market had its beginnings in the nearby Fremont neighborhood at a weekly outdoor venue featuring
crafts and collectibles. When that event grew too large, the farmers peeled off and moved a mile west to Ballard. Subsequently,
sales at the remaining stalls in Fremont took a nose dive while
the neighboring Ballard Farmers' Market grew into the most
successful event of its kind in the city. Lately, administrators in
Fremont have been bringing farmers back into their mix, recognizing that nothing draws people in quite the same way as food.

It's hard to deny that the industrial food machine domi-
nates our culinary landscape, yet in recent years, a critical mass
of people have been turning to good food as a way to preserve
our health, dignity, and traditions. This movement has grown

out of the actions and passions of a far-flung group of independent cooks, eaters, and activists and has gained traction through the words and actions of talented, motivated organizers aided by versatile communication technologies. It is impossible to mark a precise starting point for this groundswell of awareness about the importance of eating well, not least because—even in countries where industrial food became the dominant cuisine—there were always individuals and families who'd never lost sight of the importance of cooking wholesome meals from scratch. Even in the United States, the birthplace of TV dinners and fast-food franchises, fine restaurants survived in major cities, and immigrant groups embraced the abundance of ingredients, especially the items that had been prohibitively expensive in their homelands.

This was especially true in Italian neighborhoods. The families that crossed the ocean had often lived in poverty before their transatlantic journey, subsisting mainly on polenta. Many of them enjoyed meat only a few times a year when the wealthy landowners who employed them hosted feasts featuring foods that their guests could otherwise never afford. But in the United States, meat was so abundant and inexpensive that the new arrivals could eat it several times a week, if not every day. Social workers assigned to immigrant communities in the early part of the twentieth century regularly complained that their clients spend a disproportionate share of their income on food. But joyful, abundant family meals were a natural reaction to the easy availability of ingredients after many generations of not having enough.

Italian immigrants to the United States not only ate well themselves, they also taught their new compatriots about food by importing staples such as olive oil and parmesan cheese and setting up factories where they could manufacture pasta stateside.

They planted tomatoes, broccoli, and zucchini and were the first to recognize the vast potential of the fertile California valleys for growing vegetables and cultivating grapes for wine. Using the railroads laid during the nineteenth century, they built agricultural empires shipping fresh produce across the country.

When it came to fine food, however, Americans historically emulated the French. The first four presidents employed French chefs, and even up until the 1950s, most upscale restaurants served meals in the French tradition and printed their menus in that language. So it is not particularly remarkable that the woman who did the most to transform American attitudes about food also drew her inspiration from that venerable cuisine. In 1958, Julia Child became known to the American public through the weighty tome *Mastering the Art of French Cooking*, which she coauthored, and in 1963, she launched her popular television show. Child had lived in France during the 1950s, where she fell in love with the food and attended the Cordon Bleu cooking school. Along with her friends Simone Beck and Louisette Bertholle, she conceived the idea of writing a cookbook designed to make French cooking accessible to an American audience.

Never having cooked professionally herself, Child was the ideal messenger to introduce the general public to French cuisine. She was meticulous about providing instructions for complicated dishes that could be followed even by novices, starting with simple steps and building skills. Child's passion resonated with Knopf editor Judith Jones, who had herself lived in France and been transformed by its cuisine. Just as Child had never worked as a chef before, Jones had never previously edited a cookbook, and this lack of familiarity with the medium gave her the ideal perspective to help birth a book targeted to amateur cooks.

The wild appeal of both the book and the television show surprised virtually everyone involved and provided indisputable evidence that Americans had developed a collective longing for better food. Child was hardly the first American celebrity cook or cookbook author; James Beard and Craig Claiborne, among others, had laid the foundation for the popular movement that achieved unstoppable momentum as a result of her work. Part of her genius lay in her groundbreaking use of the medium of television, which was still in its relative infancy when WGBH began running her show. Her unique, iconographic status came from a convergence between the medium, the message, and the perfect moment in time.

The landscape of American food changed dramatically. At the same time that fast-food restaurants and TV dinners were becoming staples all over the country and manufacturers were making indiscriminate use of artificial flavorings, sweeteners, and preservatives, an increasing number of consumers were avidly searching for alternatives. The authenticity and integrity of the dishes that Child presented in her shows and books offered more than just flavor and nourishment. To many viewers, they represented an entire way of life that was based on taking pleasure and finding meaning in basic, everyday tasks, rather than rushing through the day and finding sustenance in the most efficient possible way.

Entrepreneurs were quick to recognize the vast potential opened up by this new interest in eating well. The American culinary awakening of the late 1960s and early 1970s provided fertile ground for food importers and purveyors of kitchen equipment. Some of these products were of genuine high quality while others were kitschy or extraneous. From the very beginning, the modern American movement towards eating well embodied two very different impulses that often overlapped; as we have seen, it grew out of a collective yearning for a better way to live, but at the same time, it was very much a product of the culture that spawned it. Not only did its jargon quickly work its way into the mouths of advertisers, but it also became a fertile medium for elitism and class conceits.

The new crop of gourmets hosted dinner parties where they dazzled one another with expensive, elaborate creations. Betty Fussell, a food historian married to a Rutgers University professor, wrote in her memoir, *My Kitchen Wars*, about the lavish and competitive suburban food culture of the 1960s, with neighbors and colleagues engaged in ongoing one-upmanship that included not only food but also wine and a drive to own the finest available cooking equipment.

At the same time that socialites and intellectuals were using food as a form of social collateral, the counterculture of the 1960s and 1970s was changing their diet with the intention of putting distance between themselves and the dominant society. For them, eating well was a matter of finding sustenance in ways that didn't harm their bodies or the planet and was also a way to spread justice and equality by making sure that everyone had enough to eat. They rebelled against the industrialization of the food supply that was responsible for the fatty, starchy, chemical laden foods whose toll on the nation's collective health was becoming evident, and they also positioned themselves in opposition to the extravagance of gourmets who spent lavishly on feasts while others went hungry. They shunned culinary tradition, developing a style of cooking based on experimentation, combining ingredients in new and unique ways, and creating concoctions that were especially appealing under the influence of mind-altering drugs.

In San Francisco's Haight-Ashbury, groups such as the Diggers, who took their name from an eighteenth-century movement in England, prepared meals and served them in Golden Gate Park to anyone who wanted or needed to eat. They used simple foods and almost always cooked with vegetarian ingredients that were inexpensive and also represented a break from the hierarchical dominant culture, which exploited some species to the point of killing them and using them for food. In separating themselves from the processed foods that were prevalent in mainstream culture, these counterculture cooks eschewed white rice and white flour, opting for nutritionally superior whole grains and also for foods that were closer to their natural states.

Whether they realized it or not, by choosing whole wheat flour over more refined alternatives, these radical eaters were also challenging longstanding class conceits dating back thousands of years to the days when it took so much labor and expense to sift out the darker particles that only the rich could afford to eat white bread. Ironically, as refined flour became available to everyone, whole wheat flour became expensive. The bran that gave it its darker color was prone to grow rancid, shortening its shelf life relative to the highly processed white alternative. By choosing whole wheat rather than white flours, members of the counterculture were rejecting both the long tradition of white bread as a food for the rich as well as the contemporary industrial norm.

In San Francisco and all over the country, food co-ops sprang up as like-minded eaters pooled their purchasing power to buy food at lower prices, procuring ingredients that were usually unavailable in conventional supermarkets and creating a model of food distribution based on integrity rather than profit. Many of these early experiments eventually failed, not least because members were too idealistic to recognize that even an enterprise based on humanist and egalitarian values had to bring in enough money and manage its assets soundly enough to be financially viable. Those that succeeded were able to successfully balance their principles with day-to-day practical concerns, but they usually underwent an evolutionary process, rejecting unsuccessful policies and eventually coming up with a new model for doing business.

Many of the young people distancing themselves from established society at this time chose to move out of the cities and settle in rural areas, living collectively and sharing food, labor, and resources. Most grew at least some of their own food with little or no agricultural experience. Of course, they used no artificial fertilizers or pesticides; these chemicals represented the aspects of mainstream culture that they rejected: the artificiality, lack of concern for health, and emphasis on quantity at the expense of quality. Many of these forays into farming were less than successful at first. Yields were disappointing, and the produce was stunted and damaged by insects.

Over time, the new "organic agriculture" came into its own as its practitioners learned from role models such as E.J. Rodale and Sir Albert Howard, who had developed techniques and advocated a more natural approach to working the soil earlier in the twentieth century. Their approach to farming was new in the sense that it represented a break from established practices, but it was actually quite ancient. Agriculturalists had grown food without chemicals for twelve thousand years before modern technology spawned the intensive, profit driven system that dominated the landscape, depleted the quality of the soil, and produced nutritionally inferior food. The birth of organic farming in the United States wasn't so much a discovery as a reawakening, a rediscovery of age-old techniques with the benefits of contemporary science to test and explain hypotheses and twentieth century communication tools to facilitate the sharing of information.

At the same time that these counterculture farmers were honing their skills, the gourmets who had avidly watched Julia Child and shopped for cooking equipment at Williams-Sonoma began demanding better quality ingredients. Child often instructed her viewers that if they couldn't find the items in her recipes at their local supermarkets, they should speak to the proprietors and ask them to stock foods like leeks, shallots, and fresh basil. Enough people did so, and the offerings on the shelves of mainstream stores began to change. Farmers found a growing, enthusiastic market for specialty produce, and importers worked to please the growing audience for well-crafted products from abroad. Many of these delicacies appealed to the natural foods crowd as well as the gourmets; they contained no preservatives, which were rendered unnecessary as producers chose high-quality ingredients and processed them with care.

This convergence between the natural and gourmet food markets was most famously spearheaded by Alice Waters, founder of the Chez Panisse restaurant in Berkeley. She opened the restaurant in 1971 after spending time during her student years working on progressive causes such as the antiwar movement and also travelling in France and enjoying the food. Like Julia Child, Waters was looking to develop a venue where she could introduce Americans to the French style of cooking and eating. While Child focused largely on technique, Waters was especially passionate about her ingredients. Frustrated that she couldn't find the right materials through mainstream sources to replicate the dishes she had loved so much overseas, she began planting herbs and vegetables in her own garden and contracting with farmers in her area.

Among her other achievements, she changed the way Americans ate salad. At the time she started the restaurant, most supermarkets and eating establishments offered mainly iceberg lettuce, a tasteless variety with a long shelf life. Dissatisfied with the available options, Waters asked a friend to send her a package of mesclun seeds from France, which she planted in her own garden. Like her role models in France, she harvested the plants when they were young and tender. As it turned out, this type of salad mix had vast commercial potential, in part because it was interesting and appealing and also because it worked well as a ready-to-eat product. Unlike larger-leaved lettuces, which needed to be torn or cut into smaller pieces that browned and wilted quickly, the smaller leaves were already bite-sized, so they kept considerably longer and could be washed and bagged to create the packaged product that is so familiar to us today.

Much has been written about the chaos that characterized the early years at Chez Panisse, the drugs, romantic entanglements, and financial irresponsibility. There was so much turmoil and red ink during the first few seasons that it was doubtful at times whether the restaurant would survive. Waters herself has been a regular target of criticism because of the idealism which often trumped practical considerations and also because she was never much of a cook. Despite the fact that her vision was instrumental in shaping the restaurant and helping to spread a culinary ethic that became deeply influential across the country—and even worldwide—the chefs who put the restaurant on the map did so largely by virtue of their own skill and creativity. Collaborators such as Jeremiah Tower and Jean Pierre Moulle certainly did the lion's share of menu development and execution, but the fact that the restaurant has retained is iconographic status beyond their individual tenures is testimony to the strength of its fundamental ideals. Waters was the dynamic spokesperson for these values, and over time, her work has been instrumental to a series of important developments, from the spread of farmers' markets and the recent enthusiasm for local and organic foods to the movement for better meals in elementary schools and university cafeterias to programs teaching organic gardening to prison inmates.

While Waters started the restaurant with the intention of replicating the flavor and feel of French cuisine, she ended up creating something uniquely American. French food relies heavily on the concept of *terroir*, or food that tastes of the landscape from which it emerged. The restaurant was in Berkeley, California rather than Paris, France, so it drew on the foods that were available in its immediate vicinity. As the restaurant generated an awareness and appreciation for well-crafted raw materials, producers became increasingly innovative, planting varieties of fruits and vegetables that they would have previously avoided because there was no market for them. The farmers who worked with Waters adopted a philosophy that was diametrically opposite to that of the factory farms that surrounded them. Rather than pumping the soil with chemicals that increased yields at the expense of nutrients and flavor, they worked to genuinely improve the ground where they planted their crops, adding rich mixtures of organic matter that sprouted tastier, healthier plants.

These farmers working to serve the restaurant community soon found common ground with the swelling ranks of counterculture growers who had rejected the toxins and artificiality of mainstream agriculture for ideological reasons. They shared seeds and information, building a thriving network that supplied their neighbors with high-quality food, eventually becoming a model for the rest of the country. The rebirth of small-scale agriculture quickly became a national movement, emerging in pockets in every state and continually improving on its own achievements. Innovators learned from colleagues in their own areas and also in distant regions.

Farmers' markets began sprouting up in cities and towns, offering new sales venues for independent growers and producers. These events grew out of a vibrant synergy between farmers, customers, administrators, and even seed companies that specialized in heirloom plant varieties. As customers showed that they were willing to try new varieties of fruits and vegetables, farmers began taking chances and growing a wider range of crops, providing a more interesting selection for cooks and also helping to preserve some of the genetic diversity which our ancestors so painstakingly developed. Market administrators grew adept at securing sites, spreading the word about their events, and reaching out to underserved communities. One especially exciting development has been the introduction of food assistance programs targeted specifically towards farmers' market sales. These include dedicated food stamp checks as well as subsidies for selected groups, such as WIC, or Women, Infants, and Children, as well as funds for low-income seniors to purchase fresh, local produce.

In 1970, there were 340 farmers' markets in the United States. In 2010, there were over 5000. The spread of these events has enabled many small-scale farmers to opt out of the vicious circle that has driven so many family farmers off their land during the past one hundred and fifty years. Rather than competing in the mainstream market on the basis of size, investing heavily in equipment, and offering prices low enough to be competitive, these growers are instead focusing on quality and flavor. They are staking out a niche in which they are better adapted than industrial farms to meet consumer needs, directing their efforts at customers who appreciate the value of labor-intensive and sustainable practices. Their produce certainly costs more than the fruits and vegetables available in most conventional supermarkets, but it is a better value because nearly the entire purchase price goes to the producers rather than to middlemen who ship and distribute the food.

As large-scale retailers began to recognize that consumers were willing to pay more for items produced without chemical fertilizers and pesticides, they began offering organic products as well. The success of the organic movement brought about a new set of problems. Some farmers chose to keep their operations small, making a living by selling a limited quantity of high-quality products. Others embraced the challenge of stepping up production to meet the growing demand. Their farms became uniform and mechanized, using considerable amounts of energy to harvest, package, and store their crops. As conventional growers began noticing the success of organic farmers, they introduced unsprayed crops of their own, monoculture without the chemicals. Some even went so far as to label conventionally grown crops as organic, taking advantage of the fact that there was no regulation in place.

During the late eighties and early nineties there was a growing consensus that the industry needed to be regulated with clear standards and guidelines. Congress asked for input from a variety of groups, ranging from small-scale activists to multinational businesses. There was a considerable clash of interests as earnest producers worked to preserve the integrity of the movement they'd founded while lobbyists fought for provisions friendly to industrial food processors. Early USDA draft legislation even proposed that genetically modified and irradiated foods could still be labeled as organic. Consumers responded with outrage, and the agency backed down. A national organic law finally took effect in 2002, and it is being continually revised. Farmers and consumers concerned with the long-term health of the land and the viability of small-scale farms advocate stricter guidelines while profit-driven businesses want them relaxed.

As organic regulations have become the domain of big businesses and government agencies, farmers and consumers have looked for alternative avenues for marketing and distributing pesticide-free produce. At farmers' markets, shoppers have the opportunity to speak directly to producers about their use of chemicals and other agricultural practices. Community Supported Agriculture is a system where consumers pay for a share of a farm's output and then receive a box of produce each week during the growing season. Like shopping at a farmers' market, joining a CSA creates a direct relationship between consumer and producer and encourages communication. Many farmers who sell directly to the public at markets and through CSA programs have opted out of the organic certification process even though they farm using organic methods. Certification is expensive. It also requires a considerable amount of paperwork. Instead of spending time and money on the right to use a label that grows increasingly less meaningful, these farmers choose to build trust by meeting customers face-to-face, speaking openly about their choices and their practices.

In other parts of the world, grassroots movements aimed at circumventing the industrial food system and preserving rich culinary traditions have repeatedly coalesced in reaction to the spread of American chain restaurants, especially McDonald's. The Slow Food movement, which has come to serve as an international umbrella for food connoisseurs and activists, was founded in 1986 following a nonviolent protest against the opening of a McDonald's in Rome. In a country where eating well is a firmly established priority, the franchise's presence symbolized a threat not only to the rich Italian culinary heritage but also to the cultural ethic of taking time to enjoy life rather than rushing through each day.

Carlo Petrini, the founder of Slow Food International, as well as its forerunner, *Agricola*, brought to the movement a particular skill for articulating his message, which can be distilled into the idea that caring about what we eat is also a matter of caring about how we live. Local chapters of the organization are called *convivia*, an Italian word for "banquet," which comes from the roots "con" and "vivia," conveying the sentiment that eating together is an integral part of living together. The organization is dedicated to preserving artisan foods unique to particular parts of the world, a commitment that it honors through its "Ark of Taste," a catalogue of traditional ingredients which are in danger of extinction.

By raising awareness and creating markets for these items, Slow Food members preserve irreplaceable foodways. The process of creating demand and export markets helps to build an international exchange very different from the homogenous international food culture being spread by multinational chain restaurants. On the surface, the rationale behind the "Ark of Taste" seems to conflict with that of local foods activists, but these two ideals are actually quite compatible. Local foods aficionados care about the distance that their food travels from farm to table, but they are also inspired by a commitment to embracing the unique fruits of their particular landscape. Like the products for sale at farmers' markets, these specialty items are created on a small scale, and they speak of traditions that favor flavor over profitability, having been passed down through families and apprenticeships. Like local foods, they help to build a community, but one that is global in its scope.

The Slow Food movement has been the target of criticism during recent years for its role in spawning a food culture primarily embraced by educated and affluent patrons. There is legitimacy to this charge, especially in light of the fact that specialty,

hand-crafted items naturally cost more than mass-produced alternatives. One of Slow Food's tenets is the conviction that eating
well is a right, rather than a privilege, yet the events it stages tend
to be expensive. To their credit, many individuals involved in the
movement have begun to question this contradiction and work
towards a more sustainable synthesis of ideals and practice.

Another well publicized confrontation with McDonald's occurred in the French village of Millau, home to a community of
sheep farmers who produce Roquefort cheese. In August 1999,
the villagers organized an action against a McDonald's under
construction in their area. This action was in part a response
to a tariff that the US government had imposed on Roquefort
cheese in retaliation for the European Union's refusal to import
American dairy products from cows fed with bovine growth hormone. In keeping with the long French tradition of treating good
food as a fundamental cultural value, these farmers attacked
McDonald's as a symbol of the degradation of the food supply
instigated by globalized agribusiness.

They methodically disassembled the partially constructed
building, loaded the pieces onto a tractor, and carted them away.
The event was widely publicized. According to early media accounts, there had been a million francs worth of damage. Later,
more thoughtful estimates put that figure closer to 40,000 francs.
The French government arrested the leaders of the action, im-
prisoned them, brought them to trial, and found them guilty. As
a result, they served short prison terms and became international heroes. The figure who received the most media attention was
a sheep farmer named Jose Bove. He was a lifelong food activ-
ist, working to establish a system of collectively organized farms
on the dormant site of a former French army base. When the

McDonald's case went to trial, 100,000 supporters assembled in the town of Millau, holding peaceful demonstrations. The defendants managed to put McDonald's on trial as well, calling expert witnesses and providing extensive evidence to support their claim that mass-produced fast food threatens long-standing agricultural traditions. They lost the court case but succeeded in raising public awareness in a dramatic fashion.

The action in Millau took place several months before the meeting of the World Trade Organization in Seattle. Released on bail and awaiting his trial, Jose Bove traveled to the United States for the occasion, taking a week before the event to travel across the country and meet with American farmers concerned about similar issues. He spoke to enthusiastic crowds of people who had heard about the action and his arrest. Like the McDonald's Corporation, the World Trade Organization was an appropriate target for the rage of people frustrated by an increasing lack of control over their own food supply. It was under the auspices of the WTO that the American government instituted the tariff on Roquefort cheese that had been the impetus for the anti-McDonald's action in Millau.

Tens of thousands of people traveled to Seattle in November 1999 to demonstrate outside the WTO meeting. The demonstrations were successful in delaying the opening ceremonies and making it difficult for some delegates to attend the talks. Due to the events outside the meetings, representatives from the poorer and less powerful countries in the organization resisted some of the more powerful nations' efforts to pass regulations strictly in their own interests. Ultimately the talks ended inconclusively, a major victory for the people on the streets. While neither the meetings nor the demonstrations were strictly about food, the

WTO's policies with respect to food and agriculture stirred especially heated reactions. Everyone eats, so policies that regulate and tamper with the food supply affect everyone.

Unlike the French bread riots of two hundred years earlier, the WTO demonstrations were made up largely of people who were reasonably well informed about the institution they attacked. The crowds in the streets of the French villages during the late eighteenth century were enraged by the hunger they experienced and reacted by striking out against rising bread prices. The people in the streets of Seattle were protesting policies that often led to lower prices as companies made themselves more competitive by moving to countries where they could employ cheaper labor and circumvent costly environmental regulations. Most of the people demonstrating in Seattle were not motivated by immediate physical needs, such as hunger, although WTO's regulations do create hunger, especially for displaced third world farmers. The demonstrators who had the resources to travel to the event expressed outrage at a system of doing business that they found morally offensive, saying, in effect, that the human and environmental cost of procuring inexpensive goods was simply too high.

Discontent over the state of international agriculture had been brewing for years, especially in the global south, home to most of the world's poorest farmers. In 1992, representatives of 148 organizations from 69 countries came together to form Via Campesina, a global movement acting on behalf of small-scale farmers fighting to keep their land and retain autonomy over their choices about how to farm and distribute the food they produce. When the United Nations staged a World Food Summit in Rome in 2002, Via Campesina held its own conference in the city in order to build support for their agenda and communicate their dissatisfaction with the way the mainstream organization was addressing the issue of feeding the hungry. The UN summit was poorly attended by top level officials from developed nations, and those representatives who did show up were largely proponents of biotech and industrial agriculture.

At the 2002 Via Campesina gathering, the organization focused on the idea of food sovereignty as a way to unify the agendas of its many constituent groups. This term expresses the conviction that residents of even the world's poorest nations have the right to control their own food supplies and are entitled to self-determination with respect to everything from choosing seed stocks to making land use decisions to rejecting processed imported items, especially those that are nutritionally inferior to traditional foods. This concept placed these groups in direct opposition to multinational trade agreements like GATT and NAFTA, which are aimed at opening avenues for large, profit-driven corporations to introduce their products wherever they please with as few barriers as possible.

This worldwide grassroots movement to preserve time-honored foodways offers a wide range of people the opportunity to continue living in ways that make sense and help to maintain their physical and emotional health. Opponents of this approach have considerably more financial and political resources at their disposal, but they lack the passion and ingenuity that comes with the drive to defend a fundamental human right.

Aftertaste: The Future of Eating Well

FROM TIME TO time, I'm asked to contribute a menu item for a dinner event aimed at raising awareness about local foods. At one of these meals, I found myself sitting at a long table in front of a plate bearing an array of local, artisan cheese. There was a similar arrangement at either end of each table, with more than thirty tables in the room. I couldn't help mentally calculating the retail value of these Tommes and Chevres, which had all been donated by small-scale producers. According to my most conservative estimate, this came to at least fifteen hundred dollars' worth of cheese. I'm deeply fond of cheese, but I never offer cheese plates as part of my own catering menus. They're just too expensive and wasteful. The main ingredient is a pricey protein, and you have to serve more than folks will eat because it looks bad to run out. You can't reuse the leftovers.

These extravagant cheese plates struck me as a metaphor for the crisis of identity and values facing today's sustainable food movement. On the one hand, we are finding our way back to a more sensible way of eating, one with long-term viability. At the same time, we are mired in the vestiges of traditional dining habits which make a show of opulence and a habit of waste. The modern groundswell of interest in well-crafted food was spearheaded and popularized by innovative chefs cooking for an audience of educated and well-off diners. It probably never would have achieved its current level of popularity without the trappings of affluence that have been associated with eating well since ancient times. But if today's sustainable food movement is going to realize its vast potential for improving the health and quality of life of a wide range of people, it will need to morph from its current image as a luxurious lifestyle choice into a practical, affordable alternative.

We are hardly the first society that has eaten ourselves into a predicament by choosing foods that make shortsighted use of our resources, opting for short-term extravagance over long-term prudence. The landscape of the Near East is littered with Neolithic sites that were abandoned because their residents failed to return enough nutrients to the soil to ensure its long-term vitality. There are ruins of unsustainable civilizations in the rest of the world as well, from the jungles of Central America to the plains of Missouri to the Easter Islands of the South Pacific. Some anthropologists and archaeologists believe that our history of using food resources in unsustainable ways goes back even further to the times when our Paleolithic ancestors hunted many large mammal species into extinction.

Today we have the benefit of modern research to develop a sophisticated understanding of the damage we are causing to our habitat, and we have advanced communication tools to rapidly spread the word. But we are up against especially formidable destructive forces as our technologies for intensive production and resource extraction are capable of doing considerably more damage than the activities of earlier ages. We understand the dangers we face, but we may or may not be proactive enough to remedy the situation in time.

Food offers us an ideal venue for fostering better ways to live. Sustainable practices for raising and handling food create high-quality products that are more satisfying than the synthetic, processed flavors on the shelves of most supermarkets. We have an ongoing, daily need for food, unlike more durable commodities like clothing and building materials; as a result, we have multiple opportunities to make sensible food choices each and every day.

Unfortunately, our tastes in food are heavily conditioned by our biology and history, which regularly sabotage us in our quest to adapt. For most of the time that our species roamed the planet looking for food, we were never quite certain whether we would find enough. The supply of vital nutrients such as fats and carbohydrates was so unpredictable that we developed a genetic predilection for them, an inclination to choose them over other available foods, particularly leafy greens. These adaptations served us well during our days as hunter-gatherers, but they hurt us today, now that we have learned to produce such a consistent, abundant supply of sweet, fatty, starchy foods that we need to correct the resulting health problems by eating fresh vegetables. The same foods that take a heavy toll on our physical well-being also mar our landscape and poison our air and water. Processed foods are made largely from intensively farmed commodity crops such as corn and soy, which are heavily sprayed and require considerable inputs of fossil fuel.

Our contemporary quest to eat well is also hampered as by our long history of class division. Aside from the biological predisposition that spurs us to reach for some items rather than others, we crave certain foods by virtue of their rarity or perceived value. Foods that are scarce or nutritionally dense have

always been disproportionately available to people at the top of
the social hierarchy. From the Paleolithic hunters who divided
their spoils—giving the most desirable organs to the most powerful members of their communities—to the medieval lords whose
tables groaned under the weight of their lavish feasts, there have
historically been deep inequities in the ways that humans distributed food. Delicacies available on a daily basis to the wealthy
and powerful held a particular mystique for families with lesser
means, for whom they marked seasonal celebrations and occasional windfalls. These tastes and preferences were passed down
through multiple generations over the course of millennia and
are reinforced today by savvy marketing professionals. They per-
sist long after the coveted food has shrunken from an expensive
rarity to an everyday staple, as with sugar, which changed over
the course of a few centuries from a scarce luxury to a working-class staple.

While medieval royalty gorged themselves on rich, fatty banquets, today's elite are flocking to restaurants focused on locally
grown, farm fresh ingredients. Their motives aren't altogether
dissimilar: in today's industrialized food economy, fresh, honest
food is at a premium, just as wild game and imported delicacies
were expensive and difficult to get a thousand years ago. Rarity
and expense add to the allure, despite the fact that the foods in
vogue today have traditionally been peasant foods, available to
virtually anyone able to keep a kitchen garden or forage in the
woods. The fact that we now cast them as upscale cuisine shows
how far we have strayed from a simple, sensible food system, and
it also suggests that our collective sensibilities are perhaps steering us back in the right direction.

Though it is discouraging to see fresh, wholesome products
priced out of the reach of budget shoppers, this contemporary
pricing fluke also enhances the appeal of sustainable foods. Just

as rare, imported spices were coveted during bygone eras, fresh vegetables today are a symbol of living well. Unlike the pricey condiments of distant ages, which could only be procured via dangerous, expensive voyages, fresh produce has the potential to be widely enjoyed, and the process of growing it improves individuals, neighborhoods, and urban landscapes. Lately, guerilla gardeners have begun planting available strips of land in urban areas, building a grassroots movement that could make fresh produce available to virtually everyone. There are agricultural projects in elementary schools and prisons, and even on the White House lawn. Community leaders and coordinators of social welfare programs are assisting in these efforts, making the connection between participating in a productive, empowering, life-affirming endeavor and eating a diet that is truly nourishing.

Just as upscale cuisine has begun to embrace ingredients that were widely available and even disdained centuries ago, we are developing a collective appreciation for international cuisines that use resources in efficient ways. The history of food exchange between cultures has always been characterized by a curious mix of xenophobia—with foreign foods viewed as disgusting or inferior—and exoticism, with select items from distant places being especially prized, not least because of their rarity. Although our newfound openness has perhaps been spurred more by a quest for flavor than by a drive to eat sensibly, the foods that have evolved in largely agrarian regions tend to make the best possible use of available materials. There is a consistent international pattern of wise and cost-effective ingredient choices, from the legume-based dhal of India to the sparing use of meat in traditional Chinese dishes to the hearty, frugal fare of the American south to the Brazilian national dish, *feijoada*, which was originally developed by slaves flavoring their black beans with pig parts that their masters discarded.

Today there is even a trend among celebrity chefs to use an animal "from nose to tail," that is, incorporating every part of its anatomy into a dish, from the brains to the organ meats to the bone marrow. Despite the bravado that frequently accompanies these efforts—the display of intestinal fortitude associated with eating foods that others may be too squeamish to try—these efforts do help to raise awareness about the importance—the veritable necessity—of keeping food waste to a minimum. Perhaps a similar consciousness will emerge with regard to the vegetable kingdom someday. It is not uncommon for enterprising cooks to use the greens from vegetables such as beets and turnips, but many professional and home cooks still peel their potatoes and apples and remove edible stems from spinach, chard, and collard greens.

Another encouraging development that has been emerging lately is a willingness on the part of farmers and consumers to experiment with parts of food plants that passed out of everyday usage during the past half century. We now see cabbage raab and kale buds offered for sale, whereas ten years ago farmers would most likely have discarded them because there was no market for them. Ironically, this trend has been prevalent at farmers' markets, where shoppers tend to be relatively affluent, or at least have chosen to make good food a priority in their budgets. This represents a break from the historical trend of poor people being the likeliest ones to make the most efficient use of agricultural resources.

A recent United Nations study found that half of all the food produced in the United States goes to waste. Not long ago, controversy and rumor circulated in the blogosphere about a Whole Foods worker who was fired for saving one tuna sandwich out of a pile that he was told to throw in the trash. Anyone who has worked in the food service industry can testify to the copious amount of waste built into the system. We have grown accustomed to restaurant portions too large for most of us to finish. Grocers find it more profitable to keep their displays amply stocked and throw away some of their inventory, rather than buying only what they are able to sell. When new deliveries arrive, they discard the older product rather than reducing its cost and running the risk that consumers will choose discounted items over others offered at full price. Food banks salvage uneaten food, but they frequently don't have the resources to pick up donations from restaurateurs and retailers every day of the week, and these businesses rarely have the space to store extra food until the pickup day.

Quite a bit of food is wasted before it even arrives at the retail level simply because it is cosmetically imperfect. Consumers are reluctant to buy produce that is wilted or damaged by insects, although these items are perfectly edible. Ironically, this customer preference for perfect produce has been one of the driving forces behind the widespread use of chemical pesticides, which cause considerably more damage to our health than the imperfections they prevent. The government of Australia recently launched an ad campaign aimed at encouraging consumers to eat fruits and vegetables that show signs of blight, in response to an especially severe drought that took a dramatic toll on the country's harvests. This approach is hardly new and unique: populations have always responded to scarcity by switching to foods they reject under more bountiful circumstances, such as vetches and wild greens. Unfortunately, these alternatives bear the stigma of being labeled famine foods. Once better circumstances return, resourceful foragers generally go back to eating their customary diets.

Unlike the famine diets of past ages, the shifts in our eating patterns that come about in the near future need to be long-term strategies rather than temporary adjustments. We need to change our thinking about the way we eat and learn to value all of the food that we have available, not just the items that are scarce, attractive, or expensive. And we need to retain this holistic perspective even if weather conditions appear to grow more favorable, or if advances in agricultural technologies artificially lower the price of food, or when we experience periods of prosperity which allow us to be fussier about our choices.

Another sensible, cost-effective way to make the most of available resources for producing food and feeding a growing global population is to reduce our meat consumption. If we lessen our demand for meat, then a greater share of our resources could go directly towards feeding humans. This insight provided the basis for Francis Moore Lappe's groundbreaking book, *Diet for a Small Planet*—first published in 1971—in which she presented the argument that world hunger is avoidable if we collectively learn to make more sustainable choices. Lappe discovered that, using an industrial agricultural model, it takes sixteen pounds of grain and twenty-five hundred gallons of water to produce a single pound of beef. There are also compelling environmental reasons for eating less meat. According to a United Nations report published early in 2008, off-gases from livestock are the single largest source of climate change, contributing twenty-eight percent of the greenhouse gases in the atmosphere, a higher percentage than even transportation.

Between 2007 and 2009, the price of grain rose considerably all over the world, in part because of growing prosperity in formerly poor countries. In a manner typical of communities all over the world since the dawn of civilization, elevated standards of living translated into an increased demand for meat, in turn using a disproportionate amount of grain and contributing to food shortages. Although the current situation has tipped precariously because of this recent improvement in living standards in countries such as China and India, their citizens hardly bear all of the responsibility. The average American eats eight ounces of meat a day, while the average person on the planet consumes three ounces daily.

On a practical level, switching to a primarily plant-based diet seems like a simple solution to impending food security crises, which will only grow more dramatic as the planet's population increases and its climate warms. But there is a strong sociological dimension to our hunger for meat, which obstructs many of our efforts to eat less of it. In addition to being a flavorful, nutrient rich food, it also has ancient, powerful cultural significance, symbolizing—among other things—wealth, power, virility, and celebration. Today we are inundated with messages encouraging us to use less energy, at the same time that we regularly see billboards and television commercials urging us to eat more meat. This is especially bizarre in light of the fact that we are also seeing an epidemic of diet-related diseases that could be controlled if we ate more plant-based foods.

Vegetarian activists have been spreading their message since classical times, thousands of years before the term "vegetarian" was even coined. Their message has always been controversial, making them the butt of jokes in the plays of Euripides and diatribes by eighteenth-century European writers on the subjects of health and national security. This situation has hardly changed today. We see Jack in the Box commercials showing a football game between teams of carnivores and vegans with the carnivores predictably trouncing their rivals, while another ad from a lunch meat company showcases a chorus of people who wave their fists in the air and shout, "Go meat!"

Considering our long and complicated history of raising, cooking, and eating meat products, it is not surprising that the contemporary marketing industry is making such regular use of this fertile material. Our ancestors developed the skills and tools to catch and dismantle small animals around the same time that they began to show some of the early characteristics that defined them as human, such as an upright gait and an increase in brain size. Later, during the Paleolithic ice ages, they used their new-found capacity to throw spears and hunt in groups to fell larger animals, ensuring their survival in a deeply hostile landscape. These advances coincided with profound cultural developments including the earliest sophisticated art, shelter, and clothing, and probably spoken language as well.

Later, among the earliest farmers during Neolithic times, in-dividuals with surplus grain were able to keep and feed livestock, earning social and political currency as they periodically sacri-ficed animals and fed their neighbors. These events gave livestock owners a special status, evolving into ancient religious customs that enacted direct relationships between the animals' owners and their gods. From medieval times down to the early modern period, meat consumption rose and fell concurrently with pop-ulation density and availability of land for grazing, but people with wealth and power consistently ate animal products more regularly. In most European lands, they were also the only ones legally entitled to enjoy wild game.

The Industrial Revolution went hand in hand with new technologies and land use strategies that made it possible for purveyors to mass-produce meat, while the colonization of vast territories in North and South America, as well as Australia, provided wide open spaces for livestock to graze. During the past forty years, the spread of factory feedlots has brought about further drops in the price of meat, so most people in developed nations can eat it every day if they choose to do so. But most of the available meat is vastly inferior to the healthy, grass-fed animals of previous generations, having little to offer in true nutritional value and being rife with food-borne illnesses.

Just as we have continued to crave salt, fat, and carbohydrates in spite of the fact that our circumstances have changed to the point that these substances do us more harm than good, we have largely kept our sense that meat is a special food despite the fact that much of the available supply is hardly cause for celebration. Vegetarian organizations, restaurants, and magazines have been increasingly popular during the past fifty years, but there is still only a small fraction of the population that has fully made this lifestyle choice, except in India where it has a long and stately history. In mainstream culture, especially in the United States, vegetarian and vegan foods have largely retained their image as bland, austere fodder, which can be traced in part to the nineteenth-century messages of fanatical proponents such as Sylvester Graham and some of the unfortunate experiments that came about before the counterculture of the 1960s truly found its culinary footing. (Some of today's imitation meat products don't help the situation either.)

Vegetarian food has evolved into a vibrant, sophisticated cuisine during the past twenty years, yet our deep, historical attachment to meat products has stood in the way of its becoming an everyday choice for the average household. Many well-intentioned converts try to make the change but end up abandoning the diet because they find it too restrictive. Mark Bittman, a journalist for the New York Times, has recently been spreading a less evangelical, more accessible message. His book, *Food Matters*, offers a persuasive, reasonable argument for dramatically reducing our intake of animal products while repeatedly acknowledging their appeal. Bittman's book offers many vegetarian recipes, as well as blueprints for meals that are not completely vegetarian but use considerably less meat than traditional alternatives.

We are also seeing a thriving market lately for sustainably raised meat and dairy, which comes from pastured animals fed organic feed and raised on a considerably smaller scale than factory farms. Beef, pork, lamb, and chicken raised under these conditions are significantly more expensive than mass-produced meat, reflecting a larger cost difference than the gap between the price of organic and "conventional" fruits and vegetables. This difference occurs largely because of the artificially low price of industrial meat as a result of the subsidies paid to the farmers who grow the corn and soy which is the basis of mainstream animal feed. Low mainstream meat prices can also be traced to the cramped conditions in which livestock are kept on factory farms. The low cost of most supermarket meat is also possible because producers externalize many of the costs of disposing of animal waste. Because of quirks in conventional accounting systems, it's cheaper to store excrement in festering lagoons than it is to compost it and use it for fertilizer.

Sustainable meat producers calculate their costs and expenses with a holistic vision of what it takes to raise and feed their animals and dispose of their byproducts. They rely on a customer base willing to pay an honest price for the food they eat. Because many of these purveyors start out on as extremely small operations, their prices are even higher than they would be if they were able to achieve reasonable, environmentally friendly economies of scale. The relatively high price of these products has helped to recreate a recurring historical dynamic: today's industrial meat is so inexpensive that it is available to virtually everyone in developed nations, but only people who are relatively affluent or willing to make difficult choices are able to afford higher-quality meat.

While this situation revives an old and difficult inequity, it also has the potential to steer us towards a more judicious diet, one which uses meat as one ingredient among many, rather than as the basis for every meal. Today's sustainably raised meat is expensive for the same reasons that animal products have historically been expensive: it takes more resources to raise meat than it does to produce plant-based foods. Honest accounting reminds us of the true cost of feeding livestock a proper diet, giving them sufficient space, and using their waste in sensible ways.

But there simply isn't enough available space on the planet to raise enough animals under sustainable conditions for people in developed nations to continue eating the amount of meat we've grown accustomed to consuming, even if livestock is pastured on marginal land that couldn't be used for growing fruits, vegetables, and grains. Fifty thousand years ago, we began eating considerably more meat as a way to survive the ice age that threatened our survival. Today our survival could very well depend on eating less meat, using wisdom and caution to opt out of the unsustainable abundance that our technologies have made possible.

This transition will involve choosing quality over quantity, a change which goes against millennia of genetic programming that helped us live through earlier periods of scarcity and unpredictable conditions. Our agricultural model needs to undergo a similar evolution. This is critical for environmental reasons: small-scale farming uses fewer toxins and preserves priceless ecosystems far more effectively than the industrial model. The tradition of independent, sensibly scaled farming is important for cultural reasons as well. Since Babylonian times, small-scale agriculture and broad-based land ownership has gone hand and hand with democratic principles and laws that protect human dignity. The Jubilee laws of the Old Testament ensured that wealth and power would not land disproportionately in the hands of a limited number of individuals, and the ancient Greeks tending the grapevines and olive trees on land that had been in their family for generations developed a political system where their own voices could be heard. The hard-working agriculturalists who cleared marginal pieces of land during the waning years of the Middle Ages signaled the beginning of the end of the repressive feudal system, and the ethic of small-scale land holdings was one of the principle tenets of Jeffersonian democracy.

Today we are seeing a resurgence of small, independent farms in the United States, even as the industrial agricultural model is as strong and environmentally destructive as it's ever been. These producers have been behind many important developments in the way we eat and think about food. They were the impetus behind the spread of organic agriculture, and now that organics have claimed a niche in the mainstream market and have been largely co-opted by profit-driven corporations, they have been able to shift our perspective so we now also think in terms of alternative certification programs, local economies, and direct sales. They have consistently worked symbiotically with chefs and entrepreneurs growing businesses that use their fine products, creating a synergy that brings us many fine foods and employs hundreds of thousands of forward-thinking individuals in work environments where they have the capacity to thrive.

The tension between truly innovative producers and more cynical companies looking to profit from the latest trend has created a confusing retail experience for consumers, but it has also spurred independent operators to be increasingly creative and resourceful. This dynamic between truly healthful foods and imitative companies with big advertising budgets goes back at least as far as the breakfast cereal magnates of the late nineteenth and early twentieth centuries, when the important insight that grains made better breakfasts than meats became the basis for an onslaught on products marketed with copycat jargon. Today the organic industry has become as much the domain of large companies who have grown convinced of its profitability, as of the visionary producers who originally set the movement in motion. Shoppers interested in truly clean items need to weed out not only foods that contain chemical preservatives but also products that disingenuously imitate the wholesome values that set the industry in motion. This has increasingly been the case as multinational food conglomerates have bought small, innovative brands and begun to mass produce foods that were once symbols of positive change.

A similar confusion has come about as consumers have begun to select for locally produced foods. Though much of the impetus for this movement has been a desire to buy products that have been handled by as few middlemen as possible, distributors have begun carrying "local" foods and wholesaling them to superstores. Definitions of "local" vary, just as there was disagreement about the meaning of the term "organic" twenty years ago. Wal-Mart uses the term for anything grown in the same state where a store is located. Some companies even ship items to distant warehouses before bringing them back to be sold in the region where they were grown, undermining the ethic of a movement aimed at reducing the distance that our food travels from farm to table.

These developments have forced sincere, innovative producers to look for new ways to communicate with customers about their practices, and they have motivated discerning consumers to develop tools for vetting available products. Some exemplary stores meticulously research every item they carry, and conscientious consumers have access to websites which map the ownership of brands that create the illusion of being small and independent but are actually owned by multinational conglomerates. Inquiring customers can also view sites set up by the companies themselves, which can give a real sense of their practices and their authenticity. Venues for direct marketing, especially farmers' markets, provide excellent opportunities to meet producers face-to-face and evaluate their operations and their integrity.

In developing nations, the need to rebuild a marketplace of autonomous producers has become a matter of cultural survival. The disappearance of indigenous foodways has taken a heavy toll on the health of communities that were fully able to nourish themselves before they were colonized. Changes in eating habits have disrupted long established customs that place food, agriculture, and mealtime rituals at the center of sustainable rhythms that have endured far longer than the industrial economy. Activists and traditional thinkers all over the world have lately begun finding a voice, developing strategies for continuing time-tested practices in spite of an international infrastructure that encourages homogenization. The group *Via Campesina* has successfully called attention to the issues and struggles held in common by far-flung communities. By sharing resources and information and recognizing the universality of their plight to preserve their uniqueness, its member organizations are transcending some of the barriers that have kept their constituents poor and isolated. From seed savers in India to workers squatting on unused agricultural land in Brazil, grassroots activists are introducing life affirming, common-sense solutions to the destructive hegemony that robs them of their health and traditions.

At the local level, the growth of micro-lending has become an important catalyst in helping small-scale entrepreneurs in developing nations to strike out on their own. This practice involves making small loans to poor individuals and families to enable them to get started in endeavors that will be instrumental in enabling them to be self-sufficient. These financial arrangements are designed specifically to meet the needs of people living at a subsistence level. Micro-lending systems operate under the assumption that borrowers whose very survival depends on the livelihood that they can create with the available funds are most likely to be conscientious about repaying the money; they only need terms and repayment schedules that take their particular circumstances into account, such as frequent, small installments.

Micro-loans are especially well suited to developing small-scale food businesses because a wide range of people have the knowledge and skills for producing food: there are many ways to excel and countless unique niches to fill. The infrastructure to set such an enterprise in motion can be simple and inexpensive, often involving nothing more than a cow or a goat or the materials to set up a basic irrigation system. The resulting income can rescue an individual or family from being subject to the whims of an economy that depends on decisions made by officials at distant financial institutions who do not have their best interests in mind. It can also help to restore traditional foodways, recipes, and practices that have their foundation in long-standing wisdom rather than short-sighted contemporary accounting systems.

Another alternative to the homogenization of the global food system is the implementation of Fair-Trade practices, which are designed to structure commerce in ways that benefit producers and growers in developing nations. Fair-Trade principles include ensuring that these entrepreneurs receive a fair price for their products and then reinvesting capital in their communities in ways that genuinely improve their quality of life, such as education and septic systems. There are a variety of organizations all over the world that certify products and producers as meeting Fair-Trade criteria. This certification offers the advantage of a label that consumers can easily recognize, much as the organic label acts as a guarantee that an item has been produced according to clearly defined standards. But the Fair-Trade system, like the organic label, is a mixed blessing. Holistic commerce can wear many faces, and certification criteria, of necessity, delineate specific priorities while excluding others. For example, in order to earn Fair-Trade certification, a company must be organized as a cooperative. There are many businesses that treat their workers well and give back to their communities without being formally structured in this manner, but these companies cannot use the FairTrade label.

Despite shortcomings of this kind, the very fact that we have such institutions and standards to critique and evaluate indicates a growing interest in good food and an increasing sophistication in the ways we choose our meals. These exciting developments have come about in spite of—or perhaps because of—a mainstream food industry that grows more adept every year at designing cost-effective, unhealthy products and imitating well-crafted, artisan offerings. Eating well today involves not only choosing foods that offer us pleasure and a sense of well-being, but also assuming a degree of responsibility for learning how these products were produced and what kind of toll they take on our health and our environment. Fortunately, there is a robust selection of available foods that are conscientiously crafted, innovative, and enjoyable, and the sustainable food movement has lately achieved a momentum that is nothing short of inspiring.

If you enjoyed this history, please blog about it, review it, tweet about it, or recommend it to a friend. Feel free to contact me at quirkygourmet@gmail.com.

Eat well.

DEVRA GARTENSTEIN is the owner of Patty Pan Grill, a favorite Seattle-based farmers' market business. She is the author of two cookbooks, *The Accidental Vegan* and *Local Bounty*, has dual master's degrees in English and philosophy, and teaches regular cooking classes. Visit her online at www.quirkygourmet.com.

References

Adamchak, Raoul W., and Pamela C Ronald. 2008. *Tomorrow's Table.* Oxford: Oxford University Press.

Alter, Robert. 1981. *The Art of Biblical Narrative.* New York Basic Books.

Anderson, Virginia DeJohn. 2004. *Creatures of Empire: How Domestic Animals Transformed Early America.* New York: Oxford University Press.

Andress, David. 2004. *The French Revolution and the People.* London: Hambledon Continuum.

Armstrong, Karen. 2006. *The Great Transformation.* New York: Alfred A. Knopf.

Balter, Michael. 2006. *The Goddess and the Bull.* Walnut Creek, California: Left Coast Press.

Becker, Ethan, Rombauer, Irma S., Rombauer Becker, Marion.

Belasco, Warren. 1989. *Appetite for Change: How the Counterculture Took On the Food Industry 1966-1988.* New York: Pantheon Books.

Berry, Wendell. 1996. *The Unsettling of America.* San Francisco: Sierra Club Books.

Bittman, Mark. (2008). *Food Matters.* New York: Simon and Schuster.

Blanning, Tim. 2007. *The Pursuit of Glory*. New York: Viking Books.

Bloom, Harold. 1990. *The Book of J*. New York: Random House.

Bober, Phyllis Pray. 1999. *Art, Culture, and Cuisine: Medieval and Ancient Gastronomy*. Chicago: University of Chicago Press.

Bottero, Jean. 2004. *The Oldest Cuisine in the World: Cooking in Mesopotamia*. Chicago: University of Chicago Press.

Bove, Jose and Francois Dufour. 2001. *The World Is Not for Sale: Farmers Against Junk Food*. London: Verso.

Brenner, Leslie. 1999. *American Appetite*. New York: Avon Books.

Brock, William H. 2002. *Justus von Liebig: The Chemical Gatekeeper*. Cambridge, UK: Cambridge University Press.

Brotton, Jerry. 2002. *The Renaissance Bazaar: From the Silk Road to Michaelangelo*. Oxford: Oxford University Press.

Bulliet, Richard W. 2005. *Hunters, Herders, and Hamburgers*. New York: Columbia University Press.

Burroughs, William J. 2005. *Climate Change in Prehistory*. New York: Cambridge University Press.

Cahill, Thomas. 2006. *Mysteries of the Middle Ages and the Beginning of the Modern World*. New York: Anchor Books.

Campbell, Joseph. 1959. *Primitive Mythology: The Masks of God*. New York: Penguin Books.

Cantor, Norman F. 2003. *Antiquity*. New York: HarperCollins.

Carson, Gerald. 1957. *Cornflake Crusade*. New York: Rinehart and Co.

Carson, Rachel. (2002). *Silent Spring*. New York: Houghton Mifflin.

Child, Julia, Louisette Bertholle, Simone Beck. (2004). *Mastering the Art of French Cooking, Volume 1*. New York: Albert A Knopf

Cobbett, William. (1822) 1979. *Cottage Economy*. Oxford: Oxford University Press.

Coe, Sophie D. 1994. *America's First Cuisines*. Austin: University of Texas Press.

Corbey, Raymond. 2005. *The Metaphysics of Apes.* New York: Cambridge University Press.

Curtis, Gregory. 2006. *The Cave Painters.* New York: Anchor Books.

Dalby, Andrew. 2000. *Dangerous Tastes: The Story of Spices.* Berkeley: University of California Press.

Debré, Patrice. 1998. *Louis Pasteur.* Translated by Elborg Forster. Baltimore: John Hopkins University Press.

Diamond, Jared. 1999. *Guns, Germs, and Steel.* New York: W.W. Norton. Diamond, Jared. 1992. *The Third Chimpanzee.* New York: Harper Perennial.

Diner, Hasia R. 2001. *Hungering for America.* Cambridge, MA: Harvard University Press.

Douglas, Mary. (2002). *Purity and Danger.* New York: Routledge.

Fagan, Brian. 2006. *Fish on Friday.* New York: Basic Books.

Fernandez-Armesto, Felipe. 2001. *Food: A History.* London: Pan Macmillan

Freedman, Paul. 2008. *Out of the East: Spices and the Medieval Imagination.* New Haven, CT: Yale University Press.

Friedman, Richard Elliot. 2001. *Commentary on the Torah.* New York: Harper Collins.

Fromartz, Samuel. 2006. *Organic, Inc.* Orlando: Harcourt.

Frye, Northrop. 1981. *The Great Code: The Bible as Literature.* New York: Harcourt Brace Jovanovich.

Fussell, Betty. (1999). *My Kitchen Wars.* New York: North Point Press.

Fussell, Betty. 2008. *Raising Steaks: The Life and Times of American Beef.* Orlando: Harcourt Books.

Gibbons, Ann. 2007. *The First Humans.* New York: Random House.

Goody, Jack. 1982. *Cooking, Cuisine and Class: A Study in Comparative Sociology.* Cambridge, UK: Cambridge University Press.

Hamilton, Edith. (1940) 1969. *Mythology.* Boston: Little, Brown.

Hamilton, Edith. (1964) 1993. *The Roman Way*. New York: W.W. Norton.

Hanson, Victor Davis. 1999. *The Other Greeks: The Family Farm and the Agrarian Roots of Western Civilization*. Berkeley: University of California Press.

Hart, Kathleen. 2002. *Eating in the Dark: America's Experiment with Genetically Engineered Food*. New York: Pantheon Books.

Hobsbawn, Eric. (1962) 1996. *The Age of Revolution*. New York: Vintage Books.

Jacob, H.E. 2007. *Six Thousand Years of Bread: Its Holy and Unholy History*. New York: Skyhorse Press.

Jones, Martin. 2007. *Feast: Why Humans Share Food*. New York: Oxford University Press.

Kamp, David. 2006. *The United States of Arugula*. New York: Broadway Books.

Keay, John. 2006. *The Spice Route: A History*. Berkeley: University of California Press.

Kelly, Ian. 2003. *Cooking for Kings: The Life of Antonin Careme, The First Celebrity Chef*. New York: Walker.

King, Barbara J. 2007. *Evolving God*. New York: Doubleday.

Kiple, Kenneth F. 2007. *A Moveable Feast: Ten Millennia of Food Globalization*. New York: Cambridge University Press.

Kriwaczek, Paul. 2002. *In Search of Zarathustra*. New York: Alfred A Knopf.

Krondl, Michael. 2007. *The Taste of Conquest: The Rise and Fall of the Three Great Cities of Spice*. New York: Ballantine Books.

Kurlansky, Mark. 2002. *Salt: A World History*. New York: Walker.

Kurlansky, Mark. 2006. *The Big Oyster*. New York: Random House.

Lappe, Frances Moore. (1991). *Diet for a Small Planet*. New York: Ballantine Books.

Lawrence, D.H. (2011). *Sons and Lovers*. New York: Buccaneer Books.

Leakey, Richard. (1994). *The Origin of Humankind.* New York: Basic Books

Levenstein, Harvey. 2003. *Revolution at the Table.* Berkeley: University of California Press.

Mallory, J.P. 1989. *In Search of the Indo-Europeans: Language, Archaeology and Myth.* London: Thames & Hudson.

McNamee, Thomas. 2007. *Alice Waters and Chez Panisse.* New York: Penguin Books.

McNeill, William H. (1963) 1991. *The Rise of the West: A History of the Human Community.* Chicago: University of Chicago Press.

Mintz, Sidney. 1985. *Sweetness and Power: The Place of Sugar in Modern History.* New York: Penguin Books.

Mithen, Steven. 2003. *After the Ice: A Global Human History.* USA: Harvard University Press.

Nestle, Marion. 2003. *Safe Food: Bacteria, Biotechnology and Bioterrorism.* Berkeley: University of California Press.

Payne, Robert. (1966) 2005. *Ancient Rome.* New York: Horizon.

Petrini, Carlo. 2001. *Slow Food: The Case for Taste.* New York: Columbia University Press.

Pollan, Michael. 2008. *In Defense of Food: An Eater's Manifesto.* New York: Penguin Press. Pollan, Michael. 2006. *The Omnivore's Dilemma.* New York: Penguin Press.

Porter, Roy. 1997. *The Greatest Benefit to Mankind: A Medical History of Humanity,* New York: W.W. Norton.

Price, Weston A. (1939) 2008. *Nutrition and Physical Degeneration.* La Mesa, California: Price-Pottenger Nutrition Foundation.

Renfrew, Jane. 2005. *Prehistoric Cookery: Recipes & History.* London: English Heritage.

Roberts, Benjamin C. 2002. *Past, Present and How We Can Survive for the Future in the Beef Cattle Business.* Pomeroy, WA: Benjamin C. Roberts.

Roberts, Wayne. 2008. *The No-Nonsense Guide to World Food.* Oxford: New Internationalist Publications.

Rombauer, Irma S., Marion Rombauer Becker and Ethan Becker. (2006). The Joy of Cooking. New York: Scribner.

Root, Waverly. 1995. *Eating in America.* New Jersey: Ecco Press.

Rosenblum, Mort. 1996. *Olives: The Life and Lore of a Noble Fruit.* New York: North Point Press.

Rudé, George. 1995. *The Crowd in History.* London: Serif.

Saggs, H.W.F. 1989. *Civilization Before Greece and Rome.* New Haven, CT: Yale University Press.

Sahlins, Marshall. 1972. *Stone Age Economics.* Hawthorne, New York: Aldine de Gruyter.

Salatin, Joel. 2007. *Everything I Want to Do Is Illegal: War Stories from the Local Food Front.* Swoope, VA: Polyface.

Sale, Kirkpatrick. 2006. *After Eden.* USA: Duke University Press.

Schlosser, Eric. 2002. *Fast Food Nation.* New York: Harper Perennial.

Shiva, Vandana. 2000. *Stolen Harvest* Boston: South End Press.

Sinclair, Upton. (2004). *The Jungle.* New York: Pocket Books.

Smith, Andrew F. 2001. *Pure Ketchup.* Washington, DC: Smithsonian Institution Press.

Spang, Rebecca L. 2000. *The Invention of the Restaurant.* Cambridge, MA: Harvard University Press.

Spencer, Colin. 2000. *Vegetarianism: A History.* New York: Four Walls Eight Windows.

Spencer, Colin. 2002. *British Food.* New York: Columbia University Press.

Strong, Roy, 2002. *Feast: A History of Grand Eating.* Orlando: Harcourt.

Symons, Michael. 2004. *A History of Cooks and Cooking.* Australia: Penguin Books.

Tisdale, Sallie. 2000. *The Best Thing I Ever Tasted*. New York: Riverhead Books.

Toussaint-Samat, Maguelonne. 1996. *History of Food*. Cambridge: Blackwell Publishers.

Wilkins, John M. and Shaun Hill. 2006. *Food in the Ancient World*. Oxford: Blackwell Publishing.

Wilkins, John, David Harvey, and Mike Dobson, eds. 1999. *Food in Antiquity*. Exeter, UK: Exeter University Press.

Zinn, Howard. 2003. *A People's History of the United States*. New York: Harper Perennial.

Zuckerman, Larry. 1998. *The Potato: How the Humble Spud Rescued the Western World*. New York: North Point Press.

CPSIA information can be obtained at www.ICGtesting.com
Printed in the USA
BVOW011242170212

283170BV00002B/1/P